CW01521323

THE ~~~~~ EEN LEAR

WOMAN IN THE MOON

Julia Pascal

THE YIDDISH QUEEN LEAR
WOMAN IN THE MOON

OBERON BOOKS

LONDON

First published in this collection in 2001 by Oberon Books Ltd.
(incorporating Absolute Classics)
521 Caledonian Road, London N7 9RH
Tel: 020 7607 3637 / Fax: 020 7607 3629
e-mail: oberon.books@btinternet.com

Copyright © Julia Pascal 2001.

Julia Pascal is hereby identified as author of these works in
accordance with section 77 of the Copyright, Designs and
Patents Act 1988. The author has asserted her moral rights.

All rights whatsoever in these plays are strictly reserved and
application for performance etc. should be made before rehearsal
to The Peters, Fraser & Dunlop Group Ltd, Drury House, 34–
43 Russell Street, London WC2B 5HA. No performance may be
given unless a licence has been obtained, and no alterations may
be made in the title or the text of the play without the author's
prior written consent.

This book is sold subject to the condition that it shall not by way
of trade or otherwise be circulated without the publisher's
consent in any form of binding or cover other than that in which
it is published and without a similar condition including this
condition being imposed on any subsequent purchaser.

A catalogue record for this book is available from the British Library.

Extracts from *God of Vengeance* by Sholem Asch reproduced by
kind permission of the Estate, administered by David Mazower.

ISBN: 1 84002 253 1

Cover illustration: Eugenie Dodd

Printed in Great Britain by Antony Rowe Ltd, Reading.

Contents

Introduction

The Yiddish Queen Lear and *Woman In The Moon* are my two American plays.

The idea for *The Yiddish Queen Lear* came out of a conversation with the producer Jan Ryan. One day in 1994 she handed me a book on Yiddish theatre, saying, 'You should write a play about this'.

The excitement of learning about Yiddish theatre was the pleasure of understanding how much Yiddish has influenced the major artistic movements of the twentieth century, and how Jewish crazy humour and the great social dramas became part of mainstream America. It took me time to link what I was reading with the Yiddish of my grandparents. In fact, the irony was that my grandfather came from Jassy, the birthplace of Yiddish theatre and so, by writing this play, I was coming full circle to my own heritage.

Today, Yiddish is often associated with sentimentality but, in fact, it was the language of the avant garde and of revolution. Yiddish culture influenced many of the major twentieth-century North American writers: Clifford Odets, Arthur Miller, Philip Roth, Bernard Malamud, Cynthia Ozick, Chaim Potok, as well as the Hollywood moguls who created the American Dream. Yiddish theatre is behind the Method, the Group Theatre, Marilyn Monroe, Marlon Brando, Mel Brooks, Gene Wilder Barbra Streisand and Woody Allen.

My fascination with Yiddish culture is the connections it has with the avant garde and the revolutionary movements, both politically and artistically. Yiddish was always free from religious dogma. Hebrew was the language of prayer, whereas Yiddish represented the world of jokes, theatre and a literature which was steeped in Jewish tradition and yet dared to criticise it, most notably in the writing of Isaac Bashevis Singer. It was Yiddish theatre which was to elevate the Yiddish language into both a popular entertainment for the masses and an art-form. A hundred years ago the Yiddish *Hamlet* was playing on New York's Lower East Side – *ibergezetst un far besser* – translated and far better! Yiddish theatre flourished as a fast-moving phenomenon in New York, South America and of course throughout Europe before Hitler's gas chambers wiped out the majority of Yiddish speakers and Yiddish culture. It was a volatile force, ranging from trashy melodrama to music hall, opera and serious political theatre.

Many of Shakespeare's plays were translated and adapted. I was keen to follow the tradition of using the framework of a Shakespearean text and transforming it into a contemporary play. Looking at a Queen Lear rather than a King gave me the chance to explore a non-traditional Jewish family where greed, selfishness, promiscuity and ambition could be explored from the female point of view. I wanted to write monstrous characters like those I had come across in my research on Yiddish theatre. Jews who were far from traditional morality and who were on the fringes of all societies. Traditional Yiddish theatre always had to be a 'three handkerchief production', offering a birth, a marriage and a death. I wanted to absorb this structure.

Woman In The Moon came out of meetings with men who had survived Camp Dora; a camp whose existence has been kept firmly out of the public eye. When I discovered that the Americans had brought over SS scientists to work on the space programme, I realised that the media star, Wernher von Braun, was worthy of examination. He exemplified the Faustian hero of the twentieth century for me. Instead of making a pact with the devil, my von Braun does a deal with God and, instead of going to hell, he is revered as a hero. Von Braun was never questioned about his behaviour as a Nazi rocket scientist.

England, France and the US were complicit in hushing up the true story of these Nazi space engineers. I wanted to show that their work still lives on in our daily lives: each time we use a mobile phone or watch satellite television.

THE YIDDISH QUEEN LEAR

dedicated to Ruth Posner

Characters

ESTHER

GAIL

RACHEL

CHANNELE

JOSEPH

SCHNECK

IRVING

ANNIE

FAYGELE

EDDIE

AUDITIONEES

WAITER

PRESENTER

TRAMP

WELL-DRESSED MAN

BEGGAR WOMAN

TWO PROSTITUTES

The action takes place in New York, between June 1939 and March 1941.

The Yiddish Queen Lear was first performed at the Southwark Playhouse on 20 April 1999, with the following cast:

ESTHER, Ruth Posner

GAIL (Gittele), Amanda Boxer

RACHEL (Rachele), Tiffany Papageorge

CHANNELE, Natasha Pollard

JOSEPH, Anton Blake

SCHNECK, Tim Levine

IRVING, Andrew Lawden

EDDIE, Laurence Summers

ANNIE, Anna Ziman

It was revised and first performed in its new version at the Bridewell Theatre on 24 September 2001, with the following cast:

ESTHER, Ruth Posner

GAIL (Gittele), Amanda Boxer

RACHEL (Rachele), Eleanor Brunsdon

CHANNELE, Vanessa Everts

JOSEPH, Jean-Pierre Thiercelin

SCHNECK, Daniel Ben-Zenou

IRVING, Matthew Dominic

EDDIE, Glenn Conroy

FAYGELE, Lesley Lightfoot

ANNIE, Phyn Nevelle

SECOND PROSTITUTE/MUSICIAN, Amy Butterworth

Design, Shanti Freed

Original music, Kyla Greenbaum

Lighting design, Ian Watts

Sound design, Colin Brown

ACT ONE

Snapshot

ESTHER in half shadow sings the American National Anthem in Yiddish. Crossfade to:

Scene 1

The audition onstage in a large New York theatre on Lower East Side. Actors come onstage to wait while CHANNELE, RACHEL and GAIL are rehearsing a song and dance routine to 'Rum and Coca Cola'.

ESTHER: *(To her daughters.)* Okay girls. I haven't got much time.
(They stop rehearsing and watch the audition. ANNIE is also onstage taking notes as ESTHER's stage manager.)
Well young men. You've got the greatest monologue ever written by the greatest writer in the English language. I want to hear what you are going to do with it in Yiddish. Channele!

CHANNELE: Yes, Mother?

ESTHER: If they haven't learnt it, it's typed up. Over there. *(To the men.)* You're young. You're the prince of Denmark. Your father's been murdered by your uncle and your uncle has married your mother. The mourners came to the house to sit shiva and they found themselves watching the widow dancing under the wedding canopy. As the son who loved his father, depressed doesn't come into it. You want the grave. You want six feet of earth on top of you. You want never to see the sun shine or the moon rise. You hate women. You hate your mother. You love her too but that comes up later. Get the idea? To be or not to be *duss is die frage.*
(Three men step forward to recite the Hamlet monologue in Yiddish. They all do it over dramatically. This is the English that they say in Yiddish.)

13

To be or not to be, that is the question
Whether 'tis nobler in the mid to suffer
The slings and arrows of outrageous fortune
Or to take arms against a sea of troubles
And by opposing end them. To die – to sleep
No more; and by a sleep to say we end
The heartache and the thousand natural shocks
That flesh is heir to: tis a consummation
Devoutly to be wish'd. To die, to sleep;
To sleep perchance to dream – ay there's the rub.
SCHNECK: Zein oder nit zein, dos iz die frage:-
Vos virdilker iz far dem mentschn, leidn
oon aroystrogn die alle feiln
un shtoysn foon dem stoorkhndikn mazl, tsi oyfheybn
die vofn kegn
a yam fun tsores un doorkh dem oyfshtand makhn
a sof fun ir?
Yo, shtarbn – einshlofn, nit mer; un kenen
in shlof zikh zogn, az es iz a sof
fun hartsveytik un foon die toyznt pogn,
vos lign in natur fun kerper, – dos
iz dokh an oproo, vos me meg im vintshn
foon gantsn hartsn. Shtarbn – shlofn:-Shlofn
un efsher zikh khloymen. Ot in vos es iz der ophalt.
ESTHER: Genug. Genug. A dank.
SECOND AUDITIONEE: Zein oder nit zein, dos iz die
frage:-
Vos virdilker iz far dem mentschn, leidn
oon aroystrogn die alle feiln
un shtoysn foon dem stoorkhndikn mazl, tsi oyfheybn
die vofn kegn
a yam fun tsores un doorkh dem oyfshtand makhn
a sof fun ir?
Yo, shtarbn – einshlofn, nit mer; un kenen
in shlof zikh zogn, az es iz a sof
fun hartsveytik un foon die toyznt pogn,
vos lign in natur fun kerper, – dos
iz dokh an oproo, vos me meg im vintshn
foon gantsn hartsn. Shtarbn – shlofn:- Shlofn
un efsher zikh khloymen. Ot in vos es iz der ophalt.

ESTHER: Oy vey. Noch ein.

THIRD AUDITIONEE: Zein oder nit zein, dos iz die frage:-

Vos virdilker iz far dem mentschn, leidn

oon aroystrogn die alle feiln

un shtoysn foon dem stoorkhndikn mazl, tsi oyfheybn

die vofn kegn

a yam fun tsores un doorkh dem oyfshtand makhn

a sof fun ir?

Yo, shtarbn – einshlofn, nit mer; un kenen

in shlof zikh zogn, az es iz a sof

fun hartsveytik un foon die toyznt pogn,

vos lign in natur fun kerper, – dos

iz dokh an oproo, vos me meg im vintshn

foon gantsn hartsn. Shtarbn – shlofn:- Shlofn

un efsher zikh khloymen. Ot in vos es iz der ophalt.

ESTHER: Bullshit. Absolute bullshit.

THIRD AUDITIONEE: What's bullshit about it? I've been practising for weeks.

ESTHER: It's old-fashioned. Schund. That kind of trashy, melodramatic acting went out in the nineteenth century. In 1917 we had a revolution. We learnt modern in the Soviet Union – ever hear of Marx? Meyerhold? Chagall? We're new. We make theatre for everybody. We are Americans. Zein oder nit zein, dos iz die frage. You've got to get inside Hamlet's head and at the same time I want to see a physical dynamic. It's not enough to have the intellectual idea your body has to live.

THIRD AUDITIONEE: That's what I was trying to do.

ESTHER: You. (*To SCHNECK.*) Young schlemiel. I love your face but I hate your acting. What's your name?

SCHNECK: Schneck.

ESTHER: God if it's Schneck now what was it before you came here?

SCHNECK: Probably Schmock.

ESTHER: How long you been here poor Schmock?

SCHNECK: Twelve months.

ESTHER: From where?

SCHNECK: From Bialystok.

ESTHER: Oh, the metropolis. And what does your father do?

SCHNECK: He's a tailor.

ESTHER: A schneider, huh. Show me how he measures a customer. Come here, Joseph. Now this is Joseph. He's been with me for ten years. Like a son to me. Now you, Mr Schneck, I want you to talk to him as your father talks.

SCHNECK: *Guten tog, guten tog.* Which way do you hang sir? To the left or the right?

(JOSEPH pushes him away.)

ESTHER: Not bad. You see when you forget acting and you play someone you know then at least, for a coupla seconds, I believe you, But Hamlet, never. The gravedigger, maybe.

SECOND AUDITIONEE: I promised my mother I'd play Hamlet.

ESTHER: Maybe for Chaplin but not for Madame Esther Laranovska. Hey you!

FAYGELE: Who me?

ESTHER: You think I'm talking to Sarah Bernhardt.

FAYGELE: I want to join your Company.

ESTHER: Name?

FAYGELE: Faygele Finkelstein.

ESTHER: My God. Even worse than Schneck. Alright Finkelstein. Let's see what you can do. Show the boys Meyerhold's Leap On The Chest.

(FAYGELE jumps on JOSEPH's chest.)

That's one of Meyerhold's biomechanical movements. Meyerhold taught us to physicalise, to use the grotesque, the startling, the extraordinary, to excite. That's what you have to do. You Finkelstein. You can start by looking at fixing the costumes. You, Schneck, come back tomorrow and prepare the gravedigger's speech.

(She takes the speeches away from the AUDITIONEES. RACHEL and GAIL look on with distaste.)

RACHEL: Schneck wasn't that bad as Hamlet but nobody's good enough for Madame. What does she think, another Thomashevsky will come walking through the door?

ESTHER: Okay you boys. I'll give you one more chance. Maybe you'll relax on it when you've someone else to

work with. Rachel, show them The Dagger Thrust.
Let's see if they can learn quickly.

RACHEL: Yes, mother.

> (*RACHEL goes off to the side with the AUDITIONEES.*
> (*GAIL does some warming up exercises and looks at ESTHER irritatedly.*)

ESTHER: I'm never going to get this cast. I don't know what to do. I've seen every Yiddish actor in town. If only Shakespeare had written Hamlet for women. Or King Lear. There are so many good actresses. But the men.
> (*She sits down onstage breathing heavily.*)

JOSEPH: What's wrong?

ANNIE: What's wrong darling? Rachel looks on in irritation.

JOSEPH: You want a doctor?

ESTHER: It's nothing. It'll pass.

ANNIE: Your heart again?

ESTHER: It beats too fast.

JOSEPH: Your heart's too big

ESTHER: And my kop's too small.

ANNIE: I'll call the doctor.

ESTHER: No. It'll pass. Where's Channele? Get water.

ANNIE: I'll go.

JOSEPH: (*Yelling.*) Channele! Wasser for mammenyu
Channele runs from one side of the stage to the other.
Call Maurice Schwartz. Offer him a thousand dollars to play Hamlet for you.

ESTHER: I can't do that.

JOSEPH: Why not?

ESTHER: I already asked. He said no.

JOSEPH: Well, put on *The Dybbuk* again. That'll bring them in. (*He plays the rabbi.*) 'Dybbuk. I order you to leave the body of Leah. Dybbuk Out!'

ESTHER: I heard The Vilna troupe are supposed to be coming with Dybbuk.
> (*GAIL comes in to help her mother. She looks fed up with her.*)

JOSEPH: Let Channa play Leah. We'll sell the tickets with life insurance.

ESTHER: We did that already.

JOSEPH: Do it again.

ESTHER: We lost thousands on the influenza epidemic. I can't risk insurance. What else can we try?

JOSEPH: Double tickets as government bonds.

ESTHER: You know anything about government bonds?

JOSEPH: I know a good joke. Little Moishe Mendelsohn was walking down the street when a large Prussian spat at him. 'Schweinehund!' rasped the Prussian. The Jew raised his hat, bowed and said 'Mendelsohn'.

ESTHER: What's Rachele doing with those schmocks? You think she can find a Prince amongst them? Gittele go and find out will you?

GAIL: Not Gittele. Gail. We're in America, mother.

JOSEPH: When's the wedding?

ESTHER: Wedding?

GAIL: (*Under her breath.*) Wedding. Why does she always repeat what's been said?

JOSEPH: Rachel's wedding.

ESTHER: Next month. Those girls are going to clean me out. After Rachel's it's Gail's. Those girls are going to clean me out. How will I pay for the theatre?

JOSEPH: (*Stuttering.*) Y-Y-Y-Y-You k-n-k-n-k-n-k-n-o-w I tried to get a job on the r-r-r-r-r-r-r-radio. B-b-b-b-b-b-b-but they wouldn't take m-m-m-m-m-m-m-me. D-d-d-d-d-d-d-damned antisemites!

Scene 2

Radio Station. Klezmer Music.

PRESENTER: And welcome to your own hour of Yiddish American radio courtesy of Dr Brown's Cel-Ray Beverage prepared from celery, sugar, fruit acid and carbonated distilled water. For your good health. L'chaim! And now instead of Eddy Cantor as publicised we bring you the two famous professors from Paris, France – Redy and Rudy!
(*Music: 'La Marseillaise'. Enter RACHEL and GAIL dressed in trousers and tails.*)

GAIL: Bonsoir mesdames et messieurs and die ganze
mizpuche. Here ve are in ze vunderful city of Paris.
Rudy ready?

RACHEL: Ready Rudy!

GAIL: Now vot vould ve study in zis vunderful city, Rudy?

RACHEL: Je ne sais pas, Redy. Vot vould ve study in zis
vunderful city. Essen? Fressen? (*She dances around.*) Give
me steak salmon, smoked salmon, herring as you like it,
there's pickled herring, plain herring, baked herring,
verstinkene herring, essen, fressen, essen, fressen!

GAIL: Ze kreplech? Ze matzo balls?

RACHEL: Ze matzo balls!

GAIL: No, you shmock. Liebe. L'amour.

RACHEL: Vy didn't you say so?

GAIL: Ze girls. Ze girls in Paris. Oh la la. Vell, vell, vell,
look at her with her little tra la la she got no need for
castanets-uh!

RACHEL: Vot a beauty. Vot is your name ma bellechen?

GAIL: (*Raising her voice and in a Yiddish/French accent.*)
Marie-Antoinette from ze Left Bank.

RACHEL: More like Miriam from Minsk. Boom Boom.
Ready, Rudy?

GAIL: Rudy ready!

RACHEL: Ready, Rudy?

GAIL: I already told you, Rudy ready.

RACHEL: You don't have to shout. We're civilised people
here. This is Paris, France, you schmock.

GAIL: Lend me twenty francs.

RACHEL: What?

GAIL: Lend me twenty francs.

RACHEL: Here's ten.

GAIL: I asked for twenty.

RACHEL: So? (*Beat.*) You'll lose ten and I'll lose ten.

PRESENTER: And now, ladies and gentlemen, we join Joe
and Shmo down in Miami, Florida.

GAIL: Vell I vos sitting on the beach last week, very hot,
isn't that right, Joe?

RACHEL: That's right, Shmo.

GAIL: Very hot and I vatch this young man getting a suntan. Well he comes for two veeks and ven he goes home he finds he is tanned all over except for vun part of his anatomy.

RACHEL: That so, Shmo?

GAIL: Yes, Joe.

RACHEL: So vat did he do?

GAIL: So he goes back to Detroit to see his boss.

RACHEL: Detroit? Ain't that where they make the cars?

GAIL: That's right, Joe. He works on Henry Ford's production line.

RACHEL: Chevrolet. Cadillac. Chrysler. You ever wonder, Shmo, vy they all start mit C?

GAIL: C is for clotz, clotz.

RACHEL: Who you calling a clotz?

GAIL: May I get on mit de joke?

RACHEL: Sorry, Shmo.

GAIL: Alright, Joe. Vell the guy goes to his boss and he says, 'boss, give me another two weeks off I just have to get back to Miami to finish my tan.'

RACHEL: And the boss said fine?

GAIL: No, Shmo, the boss said, 'vot are you doing to me? You vont to send me to the hospital?'

RACHEL: The boss is a Yiddisher Boy? You told me no Jews work for Ford.

GAIL: Joe. Just listen, will you. The boss says, 'You vant to give me a cancer in the kischkes? I've got two thousand extra cars to make in the next month and you vant another holiday!'

RACHEL: Sorry, Shmo. So vot happened?

GAIL: Vell, Joe, the guy sobbed and pleaded, he vent down on his knees and offered to work a month overtime, say, Joe, do you have ten dollars?

RACHEL: You already asked me for twenty back in Paris, France.

GAIL: That so? Vell, finally the guy offers to work six months free if only the boss will let him go to Miami. So the boss says okay and the guy returns to the beach only this time he buries himself in sand all over except for one particular piece of anatomy. Ready, Joe?

RACHEL: Ready, Schmo.

GAIL: Then vot, do you think, happened?

RACHEL: Tell me, Shmo.

GAIL: Who should come by but Sadie and Ruby on a hot summer's afternoon?

RACHEL: Rudy and Redy?

GAIL: No, Sadie and Ruby.

RACHEL: Sadie and Ruby?

GAIL: And what do you think, Joe?

RACHEL: Tell me, Shmo.

GAIL: Sadie turns to Ruby and she says. 'When I was twenty I was scared of it. When I was forty I couldn't get enough of it. When I was sixty I had to pay for it. Now that I'm eighty, it's growing wild on the beach!'

PRESENTER Thank you, Shmo and Joe. And now, ladies and gentlemen on your American Jewish Hour we bring you Levine and his flying machine.

Scene 3

The Café Royal.

The Café Royal on Second Avenue and East Twelfth Street. ESTHER and JOSEPH dance a waltz. Piano music continues through the scene as this is a tea dance.

JOSEPH: (*Over his shoulder to the waiter.*) A glayzele tay bitte. For the both of us.

WAITER: For you. With the greatest of pleasure. You know I'll never forget you playing the rabbi's wife in 'The Golem'. You were the tops.

ESTHER: You got a good memory. That was back in 1925.

WAITER: Like yesterday. (*Goes.*)

JOSEPH: (*Takes ESTHER's hands.*) You look a little tired. You never want to take a rest? Go back to see the Old Country? Moscow must be sweet in June.

(*ANNIE enters hurriedly.*)

ANNIE: Sorry, I'm late.

ESTHER: (*Goes to sit down at their table.*) He wants me to go back to the Old Country.

ANNIE: Do you want to?

ESTHER: It's not the moment.

JOSEPH: I'm worried about her health.

ANNIE: Now you mention it she is pale.

ESTHER: Stop talking about me as if I'm not here!

ANNIE: Alright, alright. But what about going back? You're a star of the American stage now. You'll cause a riot.

ESTHER: My starring days are gone. But that's not the point. (*Beat.*) I've lost faith.

JOSEPH: In who?

ANNIE: (*Correcting him.*) In whom.

ESTHER: You read anything other than Variety?

JOSEPH: Oh, the Joe and Adolf double act. Believe me, it'll never work.

ESTHER: A pact with the angel of death.

JOSEPH: Maybe it's just a trick.

ESTHER: Maybe. (*Beat.*) Joseph Dughashvilli.

JOSEPH: Stalin?

ESTHER: I had a lot of time for him. Thanks to Stalin there was a Soviet Yiddish Theatre and thanks to him we were ready to take on the world.

JOSEPH: You've never told me why you left.

ESTHER: We didn't mean to it just gradually happened. London, Paris, Buenos Airies. The whole world wanted Yiddish plays.

JOSEPH: But you became American.

ESTHER: I started to feel at home here. It's a country where chutzpah counts. Don't forget the pogroms. Their heat is still burning my shoulders.

ANNIE: Here we can play Yiddish and American. Gordin and Odets.

JOSEPH: Do you remember de heim?

ANNIE: I was ten when I came here from Poland. I remember the peasants spitting as I passed.

JOSEPH: How did you become an actress?

ANNIE: Family. My uncle was in the Yiddish Theatre there. He was arrested by the police in the intermission of a Gordin play.

JOSEPH: His acting was that bad?

ANNIE: No, schlemiel. Poland became Russia between the first and second act and they needed men for the army.

ESTHER: Sure I miss Europe. The smells and tastes are different. Sometimes I long for those smells. In Russia the sky is higher than it is here. But going back. I don't know. Hitler, Stalin makes me sick to my stomach.

JOSEPH: I left Warsaw when I was a baby. My memory is only the shushing of the language. The took me to Buenos Airies where we were always strangers. I never had a country called home. Maybe now, Moscow or Warsaw could be home.

ESTHER: Liebchen. I know you're trying to find what's best for me.

JOSEPH: If not Moscow take some of the Company and try Jassy. Find a Roumanian for Hamlet instead of these greenhorn boychicks.

ESTHER: I love it here Joseph. On the Lower East Side you look up and see all those tenements. Inside, men and women are talking. Or loving. Maybe the wife is preparing a chicken. Someone is playing piano. People are dancing. Or having a fight. And kids are being born in small, unheated rooms because there is no money for the hospital. Uptown in a smarter place, a man lights up a fat Cuban cigar. People drink bourbon, clink glasses and make plans. The Jews are talking about the Catskills. They remember going to the Red Apple for refreshments, the drive up the steep Wurtsboro Hill, they're full of angst incase the old jalopy can't make it. They read the Yiddish press. Mothers worrying about their sons who won't get married because they're too interested in socialism and unions. A man shoots himself because he's disgusted at being a union scab. He scabs to earn fifteen bucks a week to feed his wife and kids. After the funeral, the union decides to take on the family till they get on their feet. Every day there are small acts of progress. Close your eyes and listen to all those people in the street, Joseph. They are speaking Chinese or Yiddish, Italian or German. Some of them are colored and they're speaking the language of freedom. Here we

are proud and proud of all the tired and grimy people
you meet on the street, their faces lined with work, proud
because it's our sweat sweating in those sweatshops. It's
our labor that's working its ass off to make a few dollars.
And we're here building unions to get a decent buck to
feed the kids too poor to be born in hospital. If we keep
faith, the kids will eat, not only what's on the table but
we'll feed also their hearts, their brains, their souls. They
can be Jews and Americans. We'll Americanize the
Yiddish actors and the Yiddish public. A new culture full
of hope and resistance and joy. That's what we'll do,
Joseph. Isn't that right? Isn't that what we're here for?

WAITER: Dray glayzelch tay for Mesdames un Monsieur.
You vant some honig kuchen?

ESTHER: Nein, danke schayn. I'm watching my figure.

WAITER: A lot of us boys have been watching your figure
for years, Madame Laranovska.

ESTHER: Stop it you nebbish or you won't get a tip!

JOSEPH: Alright. What about London?

ESTHER: You know the first time I was in London I went
out to buy some bread, when I stepped back into the
street I was lost. All the houses looked the same.

JOSEPH: Maurice Schwartz played London, Jacob Adler.

ESTHER: Over ten years ago. No London is for small town
actors without the chutzpah to try it over here.

ANNIE: You think here a Jew would be allowed to be
President of the United States?

(*GAIL and RACHEL arrive with their fiancés. IRVING has
his arm around RACHEL's waist. EDDIE holds GAIL's
hand.*)

RACHEL: Hello, Mother. We thought you'd be here.

ESTHER: Come sit down. Irving What a pleasure to see
you. Such a handsome boychick. And Eddie!. My what a
lovely necktie. Waiter, noch a bissel tay and you can
bring that honeycake.

RACHEL: I picked the dress material. Irving likes it.

JOSEPH: I didn't think the fiancé had the right to see the
bridalwear before the wedding.

RACHEL: Superstition.

IRVING: I think it's great.

ESTHER: Rachel will look a million dollars.

RACHEL: That's right. All green and wrinkled!

ESTHER: And Gittele? I suppose you've seen it too?

GAIL: I'm Gail not Gittele. Yes, it's kinda off white silk. Well too white might suggest she's still a virgin.

RACHEL: Oh, you!

GAIL: And, as chief bridesmaid, I thought pink silk would be gorgeous.

RACHEL: I don't think pink's right. She'll look, I don't know.

GAIL: Too pretty?

RACHEL: (*Ignoring this.*) Blue. Or maybe gray?

GAIL: What about black? Then nobody will notice me.

RACHEL: Gray. You look lovely in gray.

GAIL: We'll talk about it later.

ESTHER: Yellow will do just fine.

RACHEL & GAIL: Yellow?

ESTHER: Well, if you don't like that then let the boys decide. Irving? Eddie?

IRVING: Yellow is fine.

EDDIE: Sort of sunny.

GAIL: Sort of yuk.

EDDIE: Sort of beautiful on you. (*Beat.*) Don't you think Irving?

IRVING: Girls' stuff. Doesn't matter what they wear. All the girls in this family are bobby dazzlers.

RACHEL: Is that tea ever going to arrive? (*Pause.*) You know mother. There's something you seem to have forgotten.

ESTHER: What's that?

RACHEL: Well, it's a little thing called a dowry.

ESTHER: For a modern girl you have curiously old fashioned ideas.

RACHEL: All my girl friends, their fathers give a dowry.

ESTHER: Their fathers, they're bankers or lawyers. You haven't got a father.

RACHEL: I have somewhere even if you are divorced. Where is he? (*Beat.*) You know Gail, our mother never talks about our fathers. Maybe she's ashamed.

ESTHER: Not much use to you at the moment Rachel. Your father is in the Soviet Union in Joseph Stalin's army. I don't think there are too many roubles coming your way.

GAIL: What about my dowry and my father?

EDDIE: Gail, I don't think now is the time.

GAIL: It's never the right time. Why not now?

(*CHANNELE enters.*)

Oh, you decided to come to tea, did you. We're just discussing all our fathers. Well, mother. Who is my father?

EDDIE: Gail!

IRVING: No, let's hear. She has a right to know.

ESTHER: Your father, Gail, was called Alexander Berkman. Ever heard of Henry Frick of the Carnegie Steel Corporation?

GAIL: Henry Frick. Didn't he get stabbed?

JOSEPH: I thought he was shot.

EDDIE: Shot and then stabbed.

ESTHER: That's right. Your father with Emma Goldman was behind it. Berkman served fourteen years in prison. He committed suicide in the South of France three years ago. So, you see, neither you, nor Rachel look as if you'll be getting much of a dowry.

EDDIE: We don't care.

IRVING: That's right.

ESTHER: And now we're talking business how will you boys support my girls?

EDDIE: I'm giving up singing.

ESTHER: Are you meshuggah?

EDDIE: Yes, instead of singing at weddings I'm going to be taking the wedding photos. So as long as people keep on getting married then I'll be behind the lens. Don't you worry about us.

ESTHER: And you Irving?

IRVING: Well, I'm thinking of giving up the bagel business and going into boxing.

ANNIE: Jewish world champion! Like Benny Leonard.

ESTHER: Boxing. Well. Why not. Maybe the next Olympics.

JOSEPH: Assimilation. When an American family buys a Yiddish paper the grandfather studies the Torah, the father the business articles and the son the sports pages.

ESTHER: Channele. You haven't asked about your father.

CHANNELE: You're my father. And my mother.

(*WAITER enters with tea and cakes on a tray.*)

Scene 4

The Radio Station.

The three sisters cross from one scene to another, singing 'Yuh mein tiere tochter'/'Yes My Darling Daughter' followed by 'Ich hob dich zefeel'/'I Love You Much Too Much' in Yiddish and English in front of a radio mike.

Scene 5

The Wedding.

A wedding canopy is made from four poles and a cloth. Violin and clarinet music leads to the actual wedding ceremony. ESTHER is dressed in a dress made of Yiddish newspapers ('Der Tog'). The bride RACHEL circles the groom seven times. The groom is given a glass in a napkin. He stamps on it. Everybody shouts 'Mazeltov'. JOSEPH and SCHNECK play the role of the badkhen (traditional jesters at an orthodox wedding.). The following is spoken-sung.

JOSEPH: Ladies and gentlemen! Today we are here to honor the daughter of the celebrated Yiddish actress Madame Esther Laranovska. Who can forget this Yiddish Duse whether in Shakespeare, Clifford Odets, Jacob Gordin or the great Anski? From Moscow and Meyerhold, she came to the Goldene Medine to show the Yankee greenhorns about real theatre. She's starred with the great Molly Picon in movies with Al Jolson, with Chaplin, with Paul Muni...

ESTHER: Genug, genug! Save it for my funeral!

SCHNECK: (*To RACHEL half singing.*) May you have a house and this house have a thousand rooms and each

room a thousand beds and each bed a bedbug and may a
cholera throw you from bed to bed.

JOSEPH: May you turn into a blintzer and your husband a
cat and eat you up and then choke to death so we can be
rid of both of you.

(*The two men now speak-sing the following as a routine.*)

SCHNECK: Dear Rachele our little darling
It breaks our heart to see you go
Dear Rachele little liebchen
To join your life with this sad shmo

JOSEPH: We wanted to be proud of our little girl
But instead shame will be your social whirl
Sickly children will you engender
And no soul will come their tears to mend...er

SCHNECK: From the first day of marriage may you enjoy
ill health
And talk of money well there's no wealth
Each night your husband goes out with stealth
Dirty business in dives dass mir nicht gefellt
From a boychick on Lower East Side
This poor punkele Isidore is marrying
Rachele, Rachele, Rachele! (*Mock operatic.*)

JOSEPH: No!
Many kinderlech will Rachele and boychick bring into
the world
Not many boys but plenty of girls
Now he's right and ready to tie the knot
And into a good Yiddishe family is what he's got
Rachele, Rachele, Rachele
And she's bound to improve her social position
Because she's marrying a boxer-musician
Now take a look at this beautiful bride
She's a groom's joy and pride
Who wouldn't want to stand by her side
to hold her to dance and to glide.

(*'The Anniversary Waltz' is played. JOSEPH, in lieu of a
father, dances with the bride. Everyone applauds. JOSEPH
then passes her to the groom. The newly-weds dance. Applause*

continues. GAIL dances with EDDIE. A tango is
played... ESTHER and JOSEPH dance. GAIL watches.)
GAIL: (*To ANNIE who leaves half way through the speech.*)
Look at her. With her beloved. The son she never had.
Why does she love him and not us. Because he has a
schlong? Look at her. How she laughs with him. Like a
lover. Joseph this and Joseph that. And look at him.
Looking at her with his sheep's eyes. Tangos are for
lovers not for an old woman and a young man. And on
Rachel's wedding day! Couldn't she behave for once with
a little dignity? She's lying about my father. After all
these years of silence suddenly a name. Alexander
Berkman! A fantasy. Some anarchist communist fantasy.
She wants to have made love with the Revolution. She
couldn't make it in Moscow so she comes here, and old
woman with her crazy ideas. Communism. Why doesn't
she go back if she loves it so much. Go back and take
her dancing boy with her.
(*Enter IRVING. He kisses her.*)
GAIL: Are you crazy?
IRVING: They can't see us.
GAIL: Suppose someone does.
IRVING: I told you the yellow dress would work.
GAIL: Yes well, take it easy will you.
IRVING: I'm marrying the wrong sister.
GAIL: You should have thought about that a year ago.
(*GAIL dances by herself in a semi tango movement mirroring
her mother.*)
IRVING: You're right. What am I going to do?
GAIL: (*Still dancing.*) You'd better play the model husband.
IRVING: Show me your legs.
(*GAIL lifts her skirt and he goes on his knees to kiss her.*
JOSEPH walks in on them. GAIL pulls at IRVING who
emerges sheepishly.)
IRVING: Oh, hello, Joseph. I was just...
JOSEPH: Looking for something you lost?

Scene 6

Christmas Day.

Dinner in ESTHER's apartment, 1939. EDDIE is singing 'Silent Night' in Yiddish. GAIL has a baby in her arms. ESTHER takes it and sings 'Maydele nit vayn'. (This is the classic lullaby 'Yingele nit vayn' adapted for a girl.) CHANNELE joins in.

GAIL: I'm whacked. Eaten too much as usual.

IRVING: (*Patting her stomach.*) You sure? You have an enormous appetite for such a small woman. Rachel's just as greedy only hers shows.

RACHEL: It's not fair. She's always been a pig and never gets fat. While the rest of us always moaning about food and calories. Drives me crazy.

ANNIE: (*Holding up her glass.*) To peace in Poland. And Czechoslovakia. And England.

ESTHER: More chicken anybody?

IRVING: (*To RACHEL.*) You'll want a third helping, won't you?

RACHEL: I probably should go to the bathroom. They say, if you throw up afterwards then you keep slim.

ANNIE: Rachel, please.

RACHEL: What's wrong? Do I offend your ladyship? Well, the door's there.

EDDIE: Rachel!

CHANNELE: (*Lifting the baby and trying to break this up.*) Evie sure is a beautiful girl.

JOSEPH: Why does my napkin keep sliding off my knee? (*Searches for it.*)

GAIL: If you love her so much keep her.

CHANNELE: I wouldn't say no.

GAIL: Without a husband? What would people say?

ESTHER: Stop it all of you! (*Everyone goes back to eating in silence.*) When are you two going to give Evie a cousin?

RACHEL: For God's sake, mother. Do you want to ruin my career?

GAIL: Mine's not ruined.

RACHEL: No because everyone runs around for you.

ESTHER: I said stop it.

JOSEPH: The police department say there are more murders on Christmas Day than any other day in the year.

ANNIE: I went out to buy some bagels this morning in my old schmatters. And what do you think? A car drew up with a nice young man in it. He asked me how to get to Carnegie Hall.

ESTHER: There's more stuffed helzel if anyone wants.

IRVING: So you told him.

EDDIE: Practise. Practise.

ANNIE: I gave him rough directions and then guess what?

EDDIE: What?

ANNIE: He asked for my telephone number.

ESTHER: Oh?

ANNIE: Said he'd invite me to Ratner's.

JOSEPH: I read somewhere, Ratner's serves ten thousand meals a week. Imagine. Ten thousand!

SCHNECK: The problem with eating at Ratner's is that seventy two hours later you get hungry.

EDDIE: What about the guy, Annie?

ANNIE: A good looking kid, old enough to be my son. I felt red in the cheeks all day.

EDDIE: Did you give him your number?

ANNIE: Don't be crazy. He might have been the Boston Strangler.

JOSEPH: In New York?

ANNIE: I can still see his face, the window of his automobile wound down. I was kinda sorry I didn't get to see the rest of him.

ESTHER: Shit!

ANNIE: What's wrong?

ESTHER: A tooth just came out. Just like that.

GAIL: Old age, mother. When I'm your age I'll've long retired.

RACHEL: I'll retire when I'm old. Thirty and you're past it.

ESTHER: I used to dream all my life that my teeth were crumbling. When I woke up I'd run my tongue all over them to make sure they were still there.

31

JOSEPH: (*Lifting his glass.*) Happy Jesusday, you Jewish troublemaker!

ESTHER: And now they are falling out.

ANNIE: Only one.

(*Dialogue sometimes overlaps. EDDIE takes the baby from CHANNELE.*)

SCHNECK: Shouldn't we be celebrating Chanukah?

EDDIE: What about the presents.?When do we get to open the presents?

ESTHER: I told everyone no presents.

JOSEPH: I've got a present for you.

ESTHER: No, I said no.

IRVING: I'm going to have a heart attack.

EDDIE: Me too.

IRVING: First time in world history a woman turns down a gift.

(*JOSEPH gives ESTHER a package.*)

ESTHER: From Macy's. You get rich or something?

JOSEPH: It's nothing.

ESTHER: It's watch. It's beautiful.

RACHEL: There's a diamond on it.

JOSEPH: Maybe.

CHANNELE: (*Pouring wine.*) Why is this night different from all other nights?

ANNIE: L'chaim. I give up. Why is this night different from all other nights?

CHANNELE: I don't know. Because tonight the Children of Israel escaped the plagues that smote the Egyptians?

JOSEPH: Pesach. Passover.

ANNIE: Is that when Esther saved the Jews?

ESTHER: That's Purim.

SCHNECK: (*Overlapping.*) What exactly happened at Chanukah?

JOSEPH: What were the plagues? Frogs? Lice? Snails?

ANNIE: Snails! Don't be silly!

CHANNELE: The Children of Israel were slaves.

ANNIE: We're not slaves. We're free Americans. (*A little drunk.*) Whoopee! When do the rest of us get our presents?

ESTHER: Later.

RACHEL: Annie use your napkin, you're dribbling everywhere.

EDDIE: You think the baby looks like me?

GAIL: (*Anxiously.*) Sure she does.

EDDIE: You lied to me.

GAIL: (*Quickly.*) What?

EDDIE: When we married and you knew you were pregnant, you promised me a boy.

GAIL: Oh, silly!

IRVING: Next time.

ESTHER: (*Holding the tooth.*) Tonight I see I'm finished.

JOSEPH: A little pain in the vanity that's what's bothering you.

ESTHER: Poor schmock. You haven't spoken all evening. What's wrong with you?

SCHNECK: Nothing.

ESTHER: Yes, there is.

SCHNECK: Just a girl. A girl I love. She won't see me.

RACHEL: Don't be silly.

IRVING: Schneck's in love with Rachel. He already confessed to me. Look I said, what can I do? I'll put in a good word but I ain't got much influence. I'm only the husband.

SCHNECK: It's true. The other day I saw your face in my soup. I just wanted to eat you up.

ANNIE: And I'm in love with Irving. He's going to be the champion of 1940. He's got terrific arms. Come on, show them to us.

(*IRVING takes off his shirt and flexes his biceps. EDDIE sings the first two lines of 'California, Here I Come!'*)

ANNIE: Wow! A Jewish boy built like a Cossack. (*Beat.*) (*She touches his arms.*) You promised I could go down to Gleeson's Gym with you and watch you train.

IRVING: It's no place for women, Annie.

ANNIE: All those men? Sure it's a place for women. Your wife's not jealous of an old lady like me, are you, Rachele?

RACHEL: (*Mimicking her.*) No, I'm not jealous of an old
lady like you, Annie.
(*Silence.*)

ANNIE: (*Takes a Yiddish newspaper and reads to hide her hurt.*)
Look at this in *The Daily Forward.* 'My son wants to
marry a non-Jewish girl. I like her very much. The
problem is my husband says he'll sit shiva if he marries
her and disinherit our boy. What shall I do. Support my
husband or son?'

GAIL: Don't you know it's not good manners to read the
newspaper at table?

CHANNELE: It's Christmas, Gail.

ESTHER: A tooth just like that. I am getting old.
(*RACHEL and GAIL look at one another.*)

ANNIE: A tooth, a tooth, what's a tooth? In some countries
they knock out a girl's teeth so she can do you know
what with men's you know whats!
(*Silence.*)

GAIL: You are always hanging around our mother, Annie.
You and Joseph with your vulgar jokes. Don't you have
homes to go to? You're paid, aren't you. You don't have
to be schnorrers for ever.

EDDIE: Gail! (*To everyone.*) She's tired. The baby…

GAIL: Tired? Never felt better!

IRVING: Gail, take it easy now!

EDDIE: Hey, mind your mouth, buddy! (*Moves forward for a
fight.*)

SCHNECK: You, guys. What happened to peace to all
men?

ANNIE: Time for a trick! (*Takes the baby, puts her on the
table, takes a long scarf and makes her disappear. Everyone
applauds.*)

EDDIE: Can you do it in reverse with cash? Just a few
thousand bucks to hire nannies, nurses and buy a new
apartment.

ESTHER: Money, that's all you talk about. All of you.
Well, you want money. Take it, take all of it.

GAIL: What are you talking about?

RACHEL: What money?

ESTHER: The business. The money we've made over the past twenty years. We've sweated for it. We've bought leases on theatres, we've hired secretaries, publicity agents, accountants, lawyers, we've bought costumes, insurance, posters, advertising, checked with the Fire Department, we've made promises to actors to the great New York Yiddish public. To everyone we've made promises. Well, now I've had enough. I'm old. I'm done. You can have it. You don't have to wait till I'm dead. Tell me what you want. Gittele? Rachele? Channele?

ANNIE: Have you gone meshuggah?

JOSEPH: Give! Give! Give! Why not?

RACHEL: I'll take it. We've worked for you, why shouldn't we have it? We could invest it in a club for our act.

GAIL: Yes. Something well-managed, not your crazy schemes.

ESTHER: And you, Channele? What do you want? Are you going into this club with your sisters?

CHANNELE: No.

ESTHER: Why not? You could make big money!

CHANNELE: No.

ESTHER: What do you want from me?

CHANNELE: Nothing.

ESTHER: Nothing. What have we here, ladies and gentlemen? A daughter, who wants nothing. You want nothing from this life, well, my girl, you'll get nothing. Joseph, call a lawyer. I'll get rid of it right now. Heartache I've had enough.

JOSEPH: It's Christmas Day, Esther.

ESTHER: You want me to celebrate? You think I'm the Virgin Mary? I said get me a lawyer.

JOSEPH: Today? Impossible. Just rest, you'll feel differently in the morning.

ANNIE: He's right.

ESTHER: Rest I don't need. My teeth are falling out. I'm all washed up. I can't keep going. You're right, Joseph. But it's not rest I need. I need to get rid of it. All of it, to hell with it!

(*Silence.*)

Back in twenty nine they used to throw themselves out of skyscrapers those guys who went bankrupt. Guts they had, even if their kischkes did land on the sidewalk.

ANNIE: I'll call a doctor.

RACHEL: You heard what mother said. We'll take the money for the new business. We've got a lawyer, Gail and I. Gail get the number. I'm sure he'll be able to sort this out.

GAIL: You see mother there is a club we've already been looking at near the Bowery. Annie moves to Esther

RACHEL: Don't worry. We're able to look after our mother.

GAIL: That's right. She needs her daughters, not strangers around her.

JOSEPH: Strangers?

ANNIE: Who you calling strangers?

RACHEL: Would you like a nice glayzele tay before you leave? Maybe there's a young man waiting outside to take you to dine at Ratner's?

ANNIE: Esther!

(*ESTHER is sitting still while her heart races.*)

JOSEPH: Shall I call a doctor?

RACHEL: Leave her, she's tired, can't you see?

GAIL: If you care about our mother, just go, will you.

JOSEPH: Good bye, Esther.

ANNIE: (*Sadly.*) I didn't get to give you all my presents. (*Beat.*) I'll leave with you.

JOSEPH: Goodbye, Channele, Evie, Schneck.

SCHNECK: I'll walk you to the subway.

(*GAIL looks at IRVING. JOSEPH gives her the baby. JOSEPH kisses ESTHER and leaves. ANNIE kisses EVIE and leaves. CHANNELE stands alone looking at ESTHER, GAIL and RACHEL.*
Light fade.)

End of Act One.

ACT TWO

Prologue

February 1940.

*As the audience come in IRVING is performing his boxing workout.
The radio is on in GAIL and EDDIE's apartment. We hear Jewish
American Radio which links the two scenes.*

Scene 1

GAIL and EDDIE's apartment.

*ESTHER is sitting on a chair sewing on a button badly. EVIE is in
her pram. GAIL is chopping vegetables.*

GAIL: Eddie will be back soon.
ESTHER: Yes.
   (*Enter RACHEL.*)
GAIL: Oh, it's you.
RACHEL: What enthusiasm.
GAIL: I was expecting Eddie.
RACHEL: Mother. You alright?
ESTHER: Alright.
GAIL: She's all laughs our Yiddish Eleanora Duse
RACHEL: Like mother like daughter
GAIL: What's eating you?
ESTHER: The baby needs feeding and putting to bed.
GAIL: I know. I know. I can't do everything.
ESTHER: Shall I heat some milk?
GAIL: No, you'll only burn it.
   (*ESTHER paces the room and turns the radio up.
   RACHEL and GAIL whisper.*)
RACHEL: Why is everyone so gloomy?
GAIL: She sits around. Never says anything.
RACHEL: You'd think she'd be pleased for us.
GAIL: Maybe she'd like to see the club.
RACHEL: Are you crazy? She'd empty the place.

GAIL: She sleeps all morning. Never helps me. I don't know what to do with her.

RACHEL: Have you heard from Channele?

GAIL: No.

RACHEL: You think we did the right thing?

GAIL: You wanted the club, didn't you?

RACHEL: Yes.

GAIL: She never even gave us our fathers' name. We owe her nothing.

RACHEL: She brought us up.

GAIL: You mean she didn't leave us in the street.

RACHEL: Yes.

GAIL: And all the lovers she had and all the time she left us on our own while she played the great Yiddish actress. Weren't you sick of Madame the great star? I was.

RACHEL: She looks pathetic.

GAIL: When did you get sentimental? What's the matter. We're doing fine aren't we? Full every night. You can't complain.

RACHEL: I'm not.

GAIL: If it's not gelt what is it? Are you pregnant?

RACHEL: Don't make me laugh.

GAIL: You're not sick, are you? Anything I should know? Irving alright?

RACHEL: I don't know.

GAIL: Oh, is that why you're in a mood?

RACHEL: You think it's normal, he never wants to, you know what.

GAIL: What?

RACHEL: Be sexy with me.

GAIL: All men are like that after marriage.

RACHEL: After twenty years okay but after one? What about Eddie?

GAIL: Well, almost all men.

RACHEL: Do you think he's going elsewhere?

GAIL: (*Laughs.*) Are you crazy? (*She wipes the inside of her leg.*) Maybe he's tired. Afterall he is doing two jobs, bagels and boxing training. Don't they get men to stop having sex when they fight?

RACHEL: He's not fighting, he's only training.

ESTHER: (*Picking up the baby.*) She's tired. You need to change her, feed her, put her to bed.
(*Enter EDDIE.*)

GAIL: You know something about children, Mother?

EDDIE: Hi, ma. (*Kisses ESTHER and the baby.*)

GAIL: You're late. We were waiting for you.
(*Someone whistles in the street. GAIL looks up.*)

EDDIE: Sorry, honey. I got another order. That's thirty weddings for next year. Not bad, eh?

GAIL: I'll just go down to the store for some milk. (*Throws on coat and hat quickly.*) Hold the baby and get her changed, will you. Rachel can help.

EDDIE: Sure. Just give me a moment to take my coat off, will you? I sure could do with a beer. Honey get me a beer? (*She leaves.*)

RACHEL: Take the dead weight off your feet, Eddie, and I'll get you a Bud.
(*Bring up radio volume 'Was Can You Mach S'Is America' by Aaron Lebedeff with Alexander Olschnetsky's Orchestra 1929.*)

Scene 2

The Street.

GAIL runs down the street and into IRVING's arms.

IRVING: You heard me?

GAIL: Oh, yes. (*Moves him downstage.*) Over there. If they look out the window...

IRVING: (*Hugging her.*) I can't bear it.

GAIL: I love you, I love you, I love you.

IRVING: I feel your fingers on me on all the time.

GAIL: (*Laughs excitedly.*) You know what, I was just talking to Rachel and on my lips I swear to God I nearly said 'your husband's semen is running down the inside of my thigh'.

IRVING: Oh, God, what can we do?

GAIL: When we make love it's your face I see.

IRVING: I can't sleep for thinking of you. I never touch her, you know that.

(*A TRAMP crosses to them.*)

TRAMP: You happy people got a dime for a guy with no job?

IRVING: Beat it.

TRAMP: No harm in asking, comrade.

GAIL: (*Shivering.*) He gives me the creeps.

TRAMP: God helps those who give charity.

IRVING: I said beat it pal before I call the cops.

TRAMP: (*Bitterly.*) Such generosity. May you live long life.

(*He goes.*)

GAIL: When can I see you?

IRVING: Come to the gym. There are hotels nearby.

GAIL: With my mother and the baby it's getting tough.

IRVING: Hire someone to babysit the two of them.

GAIL: You're right.

IRVING: Or get rid of your mother.

GAIL: Where?

IRVING: What's happened to her apartment?

GAIL: She couldn't pay the rent.

IRVING: I'll find a room for us. I can't risk it any more at our place.

GAIL: How long can we go on like this?

IRVING: I don't know, Gail. I just know I can't stop it.

Scene 3

The Apartment.

Crossfade back. EDDIE is drinking a beer with the baby in her arms. ESTHER is pacing when GAIL returns.

GAIL: Where's Rachel?

EDDIE: I told her to lie down in the bedroom. She doesn't look so good. You were a long time.

GAIL: Was I? Oh, shit. I forgot the milk.

EDDIE: You're getting absent minded in your old age. Mm. You smell terrific. Come over here.

(*GAIL walks to him.*)

I'm a lucky fella. Christ you make me horney. If your
ma wasn't here you know what I'd do with you right
now?

GAIL: (*Excited by having both men hot for her.*) You're nothing
but a stallion!

(*Pause.*)

EDDIE: (*Looks at ESTHER.*) Maybe I'll take a cold shower
instead, I'll put Evie in her cot.

GAIL: Okay.

(*He leaves.*)

ESTHER: You want me to make dinner?

GAIL: I'm not hungry.

ESTHER: I saw you.

GAIL: What?

ESTHER: With your sister's husband.

GAIL: I don't know what you're talking about.

ESTHER: I've known for a long time.

GAIL: That punk told you, your dancing boy, did he?

ESTHER: I've seen you. Here. When you think I'm asleep.
Like dogs

GAIL: Since when did you preach morality to me?

ESTHER: I didn't steal other women's husbands.

GAIL: Maybe you should've done, then we would've had
fathers.

ESTHER: She's your sister.

GAIL: I love it when you get maternal, thirty years too late.

ESTHER: Tell me one thing.

GAIL: What?

ESTHER: Whose baby is it?

GAIL: (*Laughs.*) Oh, that's rich. That's so rich coming from
you. Who's the father!! I love it.

ESTHER: I won't let you do this.

GAIL: You won't let me. I'm a grown woman.

ESTHER: Your cruelty is unbelievable.

GAIL: You dare say that to me?

ESTHER: I'll tell her.

GAIL: Who would believe you? You've become a crazy old
woman. Don't you know that?

ESTHER: She'll believe me.

GAIL: Prove it!

ESTHER: You are a real bitch.

GAIL: Takes one to know one.

(*ESTHER hits her. GAIL yells. EDDIE rushes in.*)

EDDIE: What's wrong?

GAIL: She's gone mad. She hit me.

EDDIE: What

GAIL: That bitch of a bitch hit me I'm telling you.

ESTHER: Ask your wife why I hit her.

EDDIE: Why did she hit you? (*Silence.*) She's got something to tell you.

EDDIE: Why?

GAIL: Because she's gone loco, meshuggah, off her head.

ESTHER: Oh, really?

GAIL: Get out of here, you, piece of dog shit!

ESTHER: Oh, I'll go alright. Nothing would give me greater pleasure.

EDDIE: She doesn't mean it.

GAIL: Don't I? Get out and never come back. May your name be wiped from the face of the earth.

RACHEL: (*Coming in.*) What's all this shouting about?

ESTHER: Goodbye, Rachel. Gail wants me to get out, so I'm off.

RACHEL: What? What's going on?

ESTHER: I've been an unwelcome guest here long enough. You, girls, have got what you want out of me. I'd rather beg in the street than take your charity.

EDDIE: Please, Mother...

ESTHER: (*Puts her hand to his cheek.*) If only I were. Poor boy. Goodbye.

(*ESTHER leaves.*)

EDDIE: But she hasn't taken anything with her. Where will she go?

(*Baby cries offstage.*)

RACHEL: Gail?

GAIL: And now she's woken the baby.

Scene 4

In front of Macy's Department Store.

JOSEPH in old tailcoat and top hat is building a shelter for the night. He is with ANNIE and SCHNECK who are also in tattered costumes from the theatre. He stops passers-by hoping for a few dimes.

ANNIE: Hey, mister. You think I'm poor. I was passing Rothschild's house the other day and in a big parlor I saw his two girls playing on one piano!

SCHNECK: Morris and Hymie were playing golf one Sunday morning when Hymie takes off his cap as a funeral cortege passes by. 'You're very respectful' says Morris, amazed by his friend's sense of etiquette. 'Well', says Hymie, 'she was a good wife'.

ANNIE: Yesterday in Brooklyn was the funeral of the richest man in the world.

JOSEPH: Really?

ANNIE: Yes, and there were thousands of people in the streets to pay their last respects. Among the crowd was a poor man in rags who was sighing and crying. Hey, you, (*To JOSEPH.*) I said to him, 'are you a close relation of the dead man?'

JOSEPH: 'No, madam, I'm no relation at all.'

ANNIE: 'Then why are you in mourning?'

JOSEPH: 'That's why!'

SCHNECK: Thank you ladies and gentleman. A dime, a dollar, a silver ring, anything will do.
(*ESTHER walks by her clothes worn-through from living rough.*)

ESTHER: Well, well, well.
(*JOSEPH runs to her followed by the others.*)
Ill met by moonlight proud schnorrers.

JOSEPH: What happened?

ESTHER: They threw me out. I've been walking for three weeks.

ANNIE: You look…

ESTHER: Terrible. I know.

SCHNECK: I thought we'd never see you again.

ESTHER: You know, I've never had trouble with my heart since I left.

JOSEPH: Really?

ESTHER: It's drowned out by the rumbling in my stomach. (*ANNIE gives ESTHER a bagel.*)

ANNIE: The delis give us at the end of the day

ESTHER: It's delicious. (*Sobs suddenly.*)

SCHNECK: What's wrong?

ESTHER: It's good to see you. (*Beat.*) Joseph...

JOSEPH: Yes.

ESTHER: I've a confession.

JOSEPH: I know. You're a secret bigamist.

ESTHER: No.

JOSEPH: You've taken up ice hockey. (*Beat.*) God forbid – You murdered your daughters.

ANNIE: Joseph!

ESTHER: I pawned the watch.

JOSEPH: It doesn't matter.

ESTHER: The watch with the diamond.

JOSEPH: Don't worry. What's a diamond!

ANNIE: (*Tries to cheer up ESTHER.*) An old woman wanted to make a match for her ugly daughter, so she goes to the rich man's son and makes a proposition. The young man is furious.
(*SCHNECK joins her in the joke.*)

SCHNECK: 'What do you mean? She's blind.'

ANNIE: 'Well' says the mother, 'that's a virtue not a fault, you can do whatever you please without her seeing.'

SCHNECK: 'But she's also deaf.'

ANNIE: 'That's wonderful', says the mother, 'you can swear at her night and day and she won't even hear'.

SCHNECK: 'And she's mute'.

ANNIE: 'What could be better? She'll never answer back'.

SCHNECK: 'And to top it all she's lame'

ANNIE: 'Call that a fault? You can run after other women and she'll never catch you'.

SCHNECK: 'But she's also hunchbacked!'

ANNIE: 'Really I can't understand you boys. With the girl you want to marry you can't tolerate even one little fault?'

(*Two prostitutes walk by.*)

ESTHER: Oh, I see you've got smart company.

JOSEPH: The girls are alright.

SCHNECK: Some are real beauties.

ESTHER: You could have a good time or catch a dose.

SCHNECK: No money.

GIRL: Can't you guys move elsewhere? This is our pitch. You're lousy for business.

JOSEPH: Next week I promise.

GIRL: Next week.

JOSEPH: If you give us a few bucks I'll make it tomorrow.

GIRL: Here then. And if I see you tomorrow, I'll call the cops – (*Realising, what she's said.*) or some friends of mine.

SCHNECK: (*Takes the dollar.*) Thanks, sister. Say, can I buy you a drink?

Scene 5

In the streets.

They walk and sing to keep warm. ESTHER sings fragments from 'Belz' and 'Rumenya, Rumenya'.

JOSEPH: Well, we got de Heim without leaving New York.

SCHNECK: Near the overhead railway line. Here. This'll do.

ANNIE: What about extracts from the great plays? We'll form a new company. 'Yiddish Theatre of the Street.'

JOSEPH: No lease to pay.

ANNIE: No actors' wages.

SCHNECK: No costumes to make.

JOSEPH: Nothing to spend. Only money coming in.

SCHNECK: What do you say?

ESTHER: No food either.

ANNIE: We'll do the delis, stock up. We can sleep in boxes. If we can get through this cold snap we'll be fine.

ESTHER: The Goldene Medine!

ANNIE: It's only temporary.

ESTHER: I'm sixty. When Jacob Adler died there was half a million at his funeral. I'll die on the street and nobody will even know.

ANNIE: New audiences every day.

JOSEPH: No taxes. No tickets.

SCHNECK: No heating, no electricity bills, (*Shivering.*) no need to buy an ice box.

ESTHER: I said I'm sixty.

(*Two PROSTITUTES stand on the corner and look at them aggressively.*)

I think this pitch has rent attached.

SCHNECK: Feh, you can smell the spunk on them.

JOSEPH: It's snowing.

ANNIE: It's beautiful. When I was a kid I went skating. My father used to watch me going round and round on a frozen lake. (*Beat.*) Once he took me to get a coat made. We went into this furrier's shop. It was full of soft skins. I pinched one. I stuffed it into my pocket like a pet rabbit. When we walked out I showed it to him. He made me go back and apologise. I was so ashamed.

JOSEPH: You never talk about your life.

ANNIE: You never ask.

JOSEPH: You been married?

ANNIE: Once.

JOSEPH: Where's your husband?

ANNIE: Last I heard of him he was touring in Chicago.

JOSEPH: An actor.

ANNIE: We're divorced. It only lasted a year.

SCHNECK: What happened?

ANNIE: I liked his family.

SCHNECK: ...And not him?

ANNIE: One day, in a drawer, I found these magazines full of naked women. And letters to girls about what he wanted to do with them. I felt bruised to the lining of my stomach. I saw inside his skull and I didn't know how to put that together with us.

(*JOSEPH and SCHNECK look uncomfortable. A train passes.*)

JOSEPH: There's a deli back there. I'll see what I can get.

(*He leaves. A well-dressed MAN passes and throws a dime at ESTHER.*)

MAN: Here, Grandma. It's cold, you should be wrapped up in bed.

ESTHER: Grandma, huh. I wuz ein star.

(*FAYGELE enters looking rough.*)
FAYGELE: I heard you wuz on the street. Can I join you?
ESTHER: It's five stars here. Sure you can afford it?
SCHNECK: Here, put my coat on. The snow is getting heavier.
(*They huddle together.*
Lights fade.)

Scene 6

The Barber's Shop.

EDDIE, IRVING, the BARBER and a CLIENT are singing a barber's shop quartet. These lyrics to 'In the Shade of the Old Apple Tree':

'In the shade of the old apfel strudel
Please come and be my noodle
How I love to google
On your doodle doodle doodle
as we schmooze far from news
you and me

I can hear the cops' sirens so mean
As my eyes turn from blue now to green
I've a face that is red
Please take me to bed
Like a lamb I'll be led
And I'll never be fed
up of thee

I need bail and I need it now
A few bucks I did take, holy cow
They will put me away
From the light of the day
And my sweet Anna May
Making hay

In the shade of the old apfel kuchen
Will you bring me a few special buchen
We can read all night long

You can play with my schlong
And we'll kiss right or wrong
Always young

In the dark of the night I first saw your tochus
I have to say my heart was filled with nachas
You're the greatest dame of all, oh yes sir
I'd like to dress you in a smart fur
It could be mink, fox or even coney
Be sure my love ain't ever phoney
I won't forget the way you first did schmooze me
Shakespeare will make it right for you and me

In the shade of the old apfel strudel
When I first saw your booble
In the blossoms as I droodle
I will yuddel for my soozel
In the shade of the old apfel strudel.'

(*The BARBER prepares EDDIE and IRVING for a shave.*
He starts with EDDIE who is nervous of the blade.)

EDDIE: Take it easy.

BARBER: Don't worry.

EDDIE: Don't worry?

IRVING: The only place you can get a little peace.

EDDIE: How's the Jewish Joe Louis?

IRVING: Never better. Roadworks every morning.
Gleeson's every night. No beer. (*Beat.*) Well, less beer.

EDDIE: And the other?

IRVING: (*Beat.*) Uh-huh. You need your energy. Of course
Rachel wants me to go back to just running the bagel shop.
All the time it's, 'I never see you, you're never home.'

EDDIE: Gail's easier going. She's not a kvetcher.

IRVING: The problem with marriage is the fun wears off. I
mean after a while what have you got to say to one
another?

EDDIE: Going to the game Saturday?

IRVING: Gotta train.

EDDIE: Can't you give it a miss? I've two tickets for the
Yankees. Most guys would give their right arm. Joe Di

Maggio! And for the Boston Redsox – Ted Williams. Just watch Joe Di hit a ball over brother Dom's head.

IRVING: Crazy that. Two Di Maggios playing on opposing sides. The Yankee Clipper against the Little Professor. Think it causes problems in the family?

EDDIE: Love and war – anything goes. Joe Di, now I'd like to see him put one in the bleachers. And Williams, he's quite something.

IRVING: Williams huh.

EDDIE: They don't call him the Splendid Splinter for nothing.

IRVING: You rate him?

EDDIE: He's gonna be as great as Joe Di Maggio! The Yankees are going to be sore they turned him down. I'd take Gail but she hates baseball.

IRVING: You could take Rachel.

EDDIE: Dames don't get it. What about you and me, front row seats, centre field watching Di Maggio track back to catch Hank Greenberg's shot?

IRVING: You making me guilty now. Tell you what, next time the Redsox play the Yankees, I promise.

EDDIE: Okay, I'll take my pa. (*Taking the towel from the barber.*) What do I owe you, buddy?

BARBER: Zilch if I can have your second seat at Yankee stadium?

EDDIE: Chutzpah you don't lack. Here's a quarter. (As he leaves.) Hey Irving, you want to come over after the club Saturday? Gail will be glad to see you. We can all drink a few beers. Don't worry. For you I'll make gin fizz without the gin.

(*BARBER shaves IRVING as EDDIE leaves.*)

Scene 7

The Yiddish Theatre of the Streets.

JOSEPH is singing 'Bei Mir bist Du Shayn'.

SCHNECK: Ladies and gentlemen. Let me present the New York début of the Yiddish Theatre of the Streets? Here you'll see works by the greatest authors on the Yiddish stage. Admired by men from Franz Kafka to Albert Einstein, Yiddish Theatre will make you laugh, cry, sing and dance. This is a three handkerchief production. One for each act. A wedding. A birth. A death. Here all life is before you in its splendid nakedness! Come and watch. You never know who that person is standing next to you. He could be your future husband, she could be your future wife.

ESTHER: It's never too late to get married!

ANNIE: Today we premiere the greatest of all Yiddish writers, the wonderful Sholem Asch.

JOSEPH: How many of you know the magnificent *God of Vengeance*?

SCHNECK: With its stories of brothels and lesbians.

ESTHER: Instead of snow imagine rain.

ANNIE: Instead of forty imagine twenty. I'm Rivkele, the young chaste daughter of the brothel keeper and I'm standing in the rain with my lover, the young prostitute Mankele.

ESTHER: Instead of sixty imagine twenty.

ANNIE: Ladies and gentlemen. Use your imaginations. You're in for a treat, the international star Esther Laranovska plays the young Mankele.

(*ESTHER does a movement wiggling her behind.*)

JOSEPH: What are you doing?

ESTHER: It's an exercise Meyerhold taught me.

ANNIE: Wagging your arse you don't need Meyerhold. It comes natural.

ESTHER: He made his actors go to the farm to watch how a female turkey moves its tail to flirt with the male.

SCHNECK: Just take a walk on Fifth Avenue.

JOSEPH: Ladies and gentlemen. The great Vsevolod Meyerhold's world famous theatre illustrated for you here now in the flesh by Madame Laranovska's celebrated Theatre of the Streets!

SCHNECK: And to enrich your enjoyment an extract from the renowned Sholem Asch's *God of Vengeance*. A moral tale from the lower depths of a Jewish brothel.

(*JOSEPH and SCHNECK shadow box as a biomechanical exercise. Scene from Sholem Asch is played out by ESTHER and ANNIE. A dumb show where MANKELE puts RIVKELE's hands on her breasts. Then MANKELE kisses RIVKELEs breasts. They kiss.*)

MANKELE: Du bis azoy shayn Rivkele. Komm zu mir. Lag dein poonim ayf mein brust.*

RIVKELE: Mein tate, er vill nikht offveken?

MANKELE: Nein, Rivkele, er vill nicht vissen. (*Kissing her.*) Es ist goot, Rivkele? Es ist goot? Du vilst mir hassene hoben?

RIVKELE: Yor, yor, Manke ikh vil.

MANKELE: Vart, vart, Rivkele, tate, mame hobenzik shlofn gelegt. Vilst du shlofn mit mir in eyn bet Rivkele?

RIVKELE: Yor, yor. Ikh vil…ikh vil.

(*They bow. No one is there.*)

ESTHER: We'll die here on this street. It's meshuggah, 'The Yiddish Theatre of the Street'! How much did we make?

SCHNECK: Ten cents.

JOSEPH: Not bad.

ESTHER: Ten cents! We'll die here unless we think of something.

* English translation of this scene on page 70.

Scene 8

The Dressing Room.

RACHEL and GAIL are getting ready and practising songs for their act. CHANNELE enters.

RACHEL: Well, well. The prodigal returns.

GAIL: What brought the cat back?

CHANNELE: I'm hungry.

(*GAIL gives her an apple.*)

GAIL: You look like shit.

CHANNELE: That's how I feel.

RACHEL: Where have you been?

CHANNELE: Looking for mother.

GAIL: You've let yourself go.

RACHEL: Forget her, will you. She'll be alright.

GAIL: Where did you look?

CHANNELE: I went to the police. The laughed in my face.

RACHEL: You tried all the theatres?

CHANNELE: Nobody's seen her for a month. (*Beat.*) I went to the city morgues.

GAIL: My God!

CHANNELE: I saw a lot of dead old women.

GAIL: And?

(*CHANNELE shrugs.*)

RACHEL: Can you still sing?

CHANNELE: After a coffee and a shower maybe.

Scene 9

The Club.

Spotlight on CHANNELE singing 'Don't Sit Under The Apple Tree' with RACHEL and GAIL. IRVING and EDDIE watch. They are drinking.

IRVING: Quite an act those three.

EDDIE: I didn't know Channele was back.

IRVING: Me neither. But she's good for business. She's certainly easy on the eye.

EDDIE: How's the training? Ready to take on Joe Louis?

IRVING: Sure. After I've finished this beer.

EDDIE: Ever think of the old woman?

IRVING: Rachel never mentions her.

EDDIE: Gail neither.

IRVING: How's business?

EDDIE: Not so good. I don't know whether fewer people are getting married or they just don't ask me to take the photos. Maybe I was naive thinking it would come easy. (*GAIL and RACHEL come over to EDDIE and IRVING.*)

GAIL: (*Kisses IRVING and EDDIE. Puts her arms round both men.*) Well, what do you think? Golden Girl's back.

EDDIE: We noticed. She coming out?

RACHEL: Don't I get a kiss? (*IRVING kisses her.*) That guy over never took his eyes off my ass. You'd think it was my ass that was singing.

(*IRVING pays no attention to RACHEL.*)

IRVING: Channele looks well.

EDDIE: She's quite something.

GAIL: She arrived looking like dog vomit. She's just
cleaning herself up. I gave her something to wear.

IRVING: That a new dress, Gail?

GAIL: You like it?

IRVING: You look terrific – (*Beat.*) – both of you.

RACHEL: You seem to like my sister one helluva lot,
Irving. Anyone'd think you two were having an affair.
(*GAIL withdraws her arms from both men. Silence.*)

IRVING: (*Laughs.*) Oh, I love you, Rachel, and most of all I
love your sense of humour.

EDDIE: Any chance of another beer around here?

Scene 10

The Street.

*ANNIE, ESTHER, JOSEPH, FEYGELE, SCHNECK are sleeping
in boxes. CHANNELE walks by and looks at the boxes.*

CHANNELE: Mother.
(*ESTHER crawls out of the box.*)
Mother. It's me. Oh, my darling, darling little mother.
Oh, God, I thought you were dead. God in heaven. Here
in the street. How could they have done this to you?

ESTHER: Joseph, come quickly!

JOSEPH: (*Coming out of his box.*) I'm dreaming. I'm
dreaming. I'm on the street with you and along comes
Channele. I'll make myself wake up. No. You're still
there.

CHANNELE: Here, take my hand. I'm not a dream. I've
been looking and looking, I kept going up to women in
the street and when they turned around it wasn't you.

ESTHER: Are you really here?

CHANNELE: Mother. Take my coat.

ESTHER: I'm so ashamed. I gave you nothing.

CHANNELE: Aren't you glad to see me?

ESTHER: I dare not touch you. I can't stand my own smell.

CHANNELE: Mother! (*Hugging her.*) I tried everyone you
knew. All the Yiddish actors have been looking for you.

ESTHER: You should have let me rot! (*Beat.*) How did you know where?

JOSEPH: Instinct. A lost kitten searching for its mother.

ESTHER: Must be the stink.

CHANNELE: I thought you were dead. I couldn't bear it.

ESTHER: You're so thin. Have you been alright?

CHANNELE: Don't worry.

ESTHER: I've no apartment, no clothes, no jewellery, nothing.

CHANNELE: I'll get you money.

ESTHER: How?

CHANNELE: I've a plan.

ESTHER: What are you talking about?

CHANNELE: Your money.

ESTHER: But how? They've put it in the club.

CHANNELE: Trust me. I'll get it back.

ESTHER: It's too late.

CHANNELE: No. I'll buy tickets to take us to Europe. To take us home. There is a boat to France next week.

(*JOSEPH imitates a French cock and overlaps.*)

JOSEPH: Cocorico.

CHANNELE: Then we'll move east. Mother, I'll take you home.

ESTHER: Home?

ANNIE: Is it safe?

CHANNELE: Joseph can see The Moscow Arts.

ESTHER: There's Annie and Schneck too. Can you buy tickets for all of us?

(*CHANNELE has gone.*)

FEYGELE: And a little space in steerage for Feygele?

Scene 11

GAIL and EDDIE's apartment.

Everyone is a little tipsy. EDDIE is humming 'We're In The Money.'

RACHEL: I never saw the place so packed! Since Channele came back we're the talk of New York.

GAIL: Where is she?

RACHEL: She went up to read to Evie and probably fell asleep.

GAIL: You guys are sure lucky having us as meal tickets.

IRVING: That's not fair.

EDDIE: Enjoy it while it lasts.

GAIL: What do you mean while it lasts!

EDDIE: Fashion. You three are tops today and tomorrow, who knows? The public is fickle.

GAIL: We're turning them away.

EDDIE: This week.

GAIL: Shit, you always spoil everything.

IRVING: Put the money where it can multiply. Wall Street.

RACHEL: At the moment it's under the mattress. Probably safer than Wall Street.

EDDIE: Stocks and shares. We come from Lower East Side. What do we know about all that?

IRVING: Find out.

EDDIE: Find out, find out when do I have time to find out? Anyway Wall Street's not so safe.

RACHEL: The Crash is finished.

EDDIE: Spend the dough. Anyway it's dames' money. Let them spend it on fur coats and fancy dresses. We earn the real money.

GAIL: Oh, yes. Wedding photography!

RACHEL: I don't know why you guys are grizzling. (*Flops out.*) It was a very good night. The best! (*She goes to sleep.*)

EDDIE: I'm going out for some more beers. (*He leaves.*) (*Silence.*)

GAIL: I wonder how long Eddie'll be gone? (*Beat.*) I can smell myself wanting you.
(*IRVING looks at RACHEL anxiously.*)
Don't worry she sleeps solid. When she was a kid she always slept like an ox.

IRVING: What are we going to do?

GAIL: Is that Channele moving upstairs?

IRVING: I can't hear anything. (*He looks over at RACHEL and then puts his hand on her leg.*) I've got your smell in my nostrils.

GAIL: I can feel you. Inside.

IRVING: Oh, God. I don't think I can stand this much longer.

GAIL: You have to. We both have to. What are the alternatives?

IRVING: We could tell them.

GAIL: Sure we could. Two broken marriages. And what about Evie?

IRVING: Gail. She's our baby. (*Beat.*) Isn't she?
(*IRVING hears something and moves away.*
EDDIE enters.)

EDDIE: Here's the beer. Shit. Is Rachel asleep?

IRVING: She's whacked. I'll let her sleep it off and then we'll get back home.

EDDIE: You can stay here. There's no problem.
(*IRVING looks at RACHEL and then at GAIL.*)

IRVING: Okay. We'll take the couch.

EDDIE: What's wrong, honey? You look all in.

GAIL: Nothing. I thought Evie was crying.

EDDIE: I can't hear anything.
(*Crossfade to streetscene.*
ANNIE has found a cowboy hat somewhere and sings a cowboysong.)

ANNIE: (*Singing.*) Ich bin nur ein Yiddish cowgirl
Just looking out to find my man
I'm just a Yiddish cowgirl
Get him any way I can

Tall or small
Homely or sehr shine
Doesn't matter honey
Long as he's all mine

Ich bin nur ein Yiddish cowgirl
Broad of brain and broad of beam
Just a Yiddish cowgirl
who likes him not so mean

Tall small brash or shayn
I don't mind as long as there's no pain
Ich bin nur ein Yiddish cowgirl
Just looking out to find my man

Oh Ich bin nur ein Yiddish cowgirl
Just looking out to find my man

(*Crossfade back to GAIL and EDDIE's apartment
Next morning. Radio is on. GAIL is cutting vegetables.*)

RACHEL: Let me do that.

GAIL: I'm glad you guys are staying for lunch. Eddie and I can't stop rowing. If you're there, it's one row less. (*Beat.*) What's wrong, you look terrible.

RACHEL: Do I?

GAIL: What is it?

RACHEL: (*Chopping.*) Can I ask you something man to man?

GAIL: Woman to woman even.

RACHEL: You screwing Irving?

GAIL: What?

RACHEL: You heard me.

GAIL: What the hell are you talking about?

RACHEL: Last night. Here.

GAIL: What?

RACHEL: In his sleep.

GAIL: WHAT?

RACHEL: He called your name.

GAIL: (*Laughs.*) Is that all?

RACHEL: What do you mean?

GAIL: Hell, you sure have imagination.

RACHEL: He called your name.

GAIL: Eddie often does that. Names of other girls all the time. Maybe Irving once had a girlfriend called Gail.

RACHEL: He was humping me.

GAIL: So.

RACHEL: First time in months and it's your name he calls? (*IRVING enters.*)

IRVING: Good morning, Gail. Sleep well? (*Silence.*) What's wrong? (*Smells his breath.*) Did I forget to brush my teeth?

GAIL: Rachel has some crazy idea that we're having an affair.

IRVING: What?

GAIL: She says you called out my name in your sleep.

IRVING: What? You crazy?

RACHEL: I heard you.

IRVING: First the mother and now the daughter.

RACHEL: No, not actually in your sleep, more when you were screwing me.

IRVING: You sick or something?

RACHEL: I say screwing. It certainly wasn't making love. (*EVIE cries.*)

GAIL: Oh, the baby.

IRVING: Now you woke the baby with your meshuggenah ideas.

RACHEL: (*Chopping.*) Is that all you have to say?

IRVING: I'm sorry, Gail, I think we should go.

RACHEL: Go? Go? I'm not going anywhere. You, you, you're a huge endless mouth. You want everything. Cake. And eat it. (*Beat.*) And fuck it too. (*Pause.*) You're both going to answer me if it's the last thing you do. (*Silence.*) You're screwing my sister, aren't you?

IRVING: Sure. I'm screwing your sister. Your mother. The baby. You name it. If it's female I'm screwing.
(*RACHEL takes the knife and goes for IRVING. He wrenches it from her.*)

IRVING: Jesus Christ, what's wrong with you, Rachel?

GAIL: Rachel!

RACHEL: You filthy, verstinkene bastard. My own sister. Couldn't you find a whore. No. Here in my own family. You yenzer!

IRVING: Stop it!

RACHEL: I'll kill the both of you so help me God.

IRVING: Rachel, darling, just calm down will you.

RACHEL: Don't patronise me you schmock.
(*CHANNAH bursts in with the baby who's crying.*)

CHANNAH: I can't get her to stop. (*Sees the situation.*) Oh...

IRVING: Jesus Christ.

(*EDDIE comes down.*)

EDDIE: What the hell's going on here?

IRVING: Call a doctor will you. Rachel needs a
    tranquilliser.

RACHEL: The hell I do. Channah take Evie. (*Puts on hat
    and coat.*) I'll just run upstairs for my bag and I'll get Dr
    Schwartz.

GAIL: I'll go with you.

CHANNELE: No, you stay here. I'll only be a couple of
    minutes.

ACT THREE

Scene 1

The street.

SCHNECK and JOSEPH stand either side of the stage in tailcoats and top hats. JOSEPH makes the sound of a ship's hooter. They are practising for when they get to France.

FEYGELE: Imagine this wooden O is not New York City but transport yourself in your mind to Paris France.

SCHNECK: Bonjour, ladies and gentlemen. To entertain you, dames and messieurs, we've come all the way from New York City. Tonight for only a coup de rouge, we make our European début in this world famous Club Clandestin. You, our audience, are la crème de la crème. Generous Jews, charming Communists, gregarious gypsies. Men loving men, women loving women. You poor, you downtrodden, lend me your ears, because here in la belle France, they are all honourable men. Nicht wahr? Bienvenue, ladies and gentlemen. Redy Rudy?

JOSEPH: Rudy ready.

SCHNECK: Hey, Rudy, you hear about the martian who dropped in on Second Avenue?

JOSEPH: No, Redy, I didn't hear that one.

SCHNECK: Well, Rudy, he goes into a bread shop and he says to the guy behind the counter 'Hey buddy, tell me, what are those wheels you selling?'

JOSEPH: Wheels? Redy? Did you say wheels?

SCHNECK: That's right. Rudy. Now this baker he says, 'They're not wheels, they're bagels' and he pops one into the Martian's mouth. And you know what Rudy?

JOSEPH: What? Redy?

SCHNECK: The martian licks his lips with pleasure and says. 'Hey you know this would go just great with cream cheese and lox!'
(JOSEPH whistles 'la Marseillaise'.)

SCHNECK: Isn't that the Marseillaise Rudy?

JOSEPH: That's right Redy.

SCHNECK: So we are in France, Rudy?

JOSEPH: That's right, Redy.

SCHNECK: Don't you owe me twenty francs from the last time?

(*JOSEPH turns out his empty pockets.*)

SCHNECK: Want to see gay Paree, Rudy?

JOSEPH: Das ist richtig, Redy.

SCHNECK: Vy are you talking German? Ve are in France.

JOSEPH: Richtig, Redy.

SCHNECK: Mein Gott, speak in French, dummkopf. 'Je suis un idiot. Tu es un idiot. Nous sommes tous des idiots'.

JOSEPH: Jawohl, mein Herr.

SCHNECK: Vot ist die matter mit du? Parlez-vous français?

JOSEPH: Jawohl.

SCHNECK: And in France ze natives speak französisch.

(*JOSEPH sneezes.*)

Gesundheit! Damnit you've got me doing it now.

(*JOSEPH starts to sing the American national anthem.*)

You came all the way from America?

(*JOSEPH does a mime of the Folies Bergeres.*)

Just to see ze girls in Paree?

(*JOSEPH nods then becomes a flirty girl in a beret who suddenly starts to goosestep.*)

Oh, I see. The girls prefer a bit of lebensraum or is that leberwurst? Anyway they are eating the German sausage. Is that what you are saying?

(*JOSEPH, as a girl, simpers and then gives the Hitler salute.*)

And that's why you speak German?

(*JOSEPH applauds SCHNECK. JOSEPH hides behind SCHNECK and puts a yellow star on his coat.*)

So the Germans like the Jews so much they are collecting them?

(*The audience sees only JOSEPH's white gloved hand on SCHNECK's shoulder as if he is arresting him. JOSEPH does a prat fall.*)

And now you schnorrers everywhere, let's have a big round of applause for Miss Channele Laranovska all the way from New York.

(*CHANNELE gives a slow handclap.*)

CHANNELE: Alright. I didn't get the tickets. Is it my fault the Germans invaded France? Consider I did you all a favour.

ESTHER: Max Ernst and Marc Chagall got out. Do you think Chagall would design for our next production?

JOSEPH: Next production? (*Bitterly.*) What will that be? The Ziegfield Follies? In Yiddish?

ESTHER: We'll go to Europe and fight.

SCHNECK: Roosevelt says we're neutral.

ESTHER: He'll change his mind. I'll tell him.

(*She appears to falter.*)

SCHNECK: Can't we get her to a doctor?

CHANNELE: Darling mother. I'll look after you.

(*ESTHER ignores CHANNELE and appears to be losing her mind.*)

ESTHER: Ride a cock horse to Banbury Cross.

(*Sings Desdemona's song from 'Othello'.*)

'The poor soul sat sighing, by a sycamore tree, sing oh, the green willow, her hand on her bosom her head on her knee.' (*To CHANNELE thinking she is GAIL.*) She's your sister!

SCHNECK: Annie. Look after her will you.

(*ANNIE arrives and the others move away.*)

ANNIE: Shall I tell you something I never told anyone in the world? (*Gives ESTHER an apple.*) When I was a little girl at school, I put my fingers down my pants. I turned to the cute little boy sitting next to me and held my fingers to his nose – here smell this! (*Laughs like a little girl.*)

ESTHER: What did he do?

ANNIE: Looked surprised. (*Beat.*) Your turn.

ESTHER: You don't know how I miss the weight of a man on top of me. Making the two backed beast.

ANNIE: (*Beat.*) Irving, he I could have handled.

ESTHER: Prize stud. Yentzer. Both my girls. (*Beat.*) Is there anything else to eat?

(*ANNIE shakes her head.*)

I wanted to go to France. In France we could eat.

ANNIE: You are right. (*Beat.*) We are French after all.

ESTHER: How are we French?

ANNIE: Before Russia where were we?

ESTHER: I don't know.

ANNIE: King Edward threw us out of England. We went to France. We were eating good cheese and drinking good wine for hundreds of years. (*Beat.*) Before the Crusades drove us east.

ESTHER: I'm tired of schlepping. Why don't we go to Macy's? Or Bloomingdale's? Keep warm.

ANNIE: The king of France is in cahoots with the bosche.

ESTHER: There isn't a king of France.

ANNIE :The president then.

ESTHER: There isn't a president. There's some Marshall.

ANNIE: Like the Wild West?

ESTHER: Army marshall. You know. Flanders. The Somme. Verdun.

ANNIE: Whenever there's a guy in charge that's what he does. Edward. Hitler. This guy Marshall. Best to have nobody in charge. Better for the Jews.

ESTHER: Those bitches. I wish to God they'd died in the womb. May they rot in hell.

(*ANNIE blows her nose and examines the snot.*)

ANNIE Filth. Nothing but filth. All I have is filth in me.

ESTHER: It's good clean Lower East Side filth.

ANNIE: (*Dissecting the snot.*) This is really vintage snot. That's from standing on Brooklyn Bridge watching freight come in. That's the Parachute Jumps at Steeplechase Park with Channele. That's from walking by Schaefer's Brewery on Kent Avenue. That's the intersection of Fulton Street and Flatbush Avenue on the way to Junior's six months ago when I met you for cheesecake.

ESTHER: I love this dreck, the stink of the street, the sound of the cars, the steam from the subway.

ANNIE: We'll go to France as soon as the Germans leave. We'll start the Yiddish theatre of Pigalle.

ESTHER: You think so?

ANNIE: There's so many Jews in France. We won't need to sell insurance to get audience.

ESTHER: I've got sulphur in my mouth.

Scene 2

The Club.

GAIL, CHANNELE and RACHEL are singing 'My Yiddisher Momma'. At the end of the song, RACHEL appears to embrace GAIL. She stabs her. RACHEL moves away quickly. GAIL slumps to the floor. Sound of police sirens.

Scene 3

CHANNELE, JOSEPH, ESTHER, ANNIE and SCHNECK are walking.

CHANNELE: I had a strange dream last night.

SCHNECK: Maybe one day we'll get some money and you and I can go to Coney Island together.

CHANNELE: I was back in the garden we played in as kids. Back in Moscow. There was a tree I loved. A poplar reaching up to God. In Russia the sky is higher than anywhere else in the world. (*Beat.*) I went back to the house but there were other people living in it. They didn't see me. As if I was a ghost. And I went to look for the tree. And there was nothing. Only a large scorched circle engraved deep into the earth.

SCHNECK: I don't remember the Old Country. Well, sometimes, there are smells. Or faces.

CHANNELE: Faces?

SCHNECK: Your face.

CHANNELE: What about my face?

SCHNECK: Well, I don't know what to say.

CHANNELE: What?

SCHNECK: Sometimes, I too have dreams.

CHANNELE: What dreams?

SCHNECK: No.

CHANNELE: Go on.

SCHNECK: You'll only laugh.

CHANNELE: Hollywood?

SCHNECK: No.

CHANNELE: What? You know I hate secrets.

SCHNECK: I dream of you.

CHANNELE: That's a nightmare.

SCHNECK: Please, Channele, I'm not joking.

CHANNELE: You are a good man.

SCHNECK: Nobody ever called me a man before.
(*Silence.*)
I feel such an ache when I'm near you.

CHANNELE: Then I'll go away.

SCHNECK: I'm in love with you, Channele.

CHANNELE: What?

SCHNECK: There. It's out. I don't care. I hate secrets too.
When I'm near you, I can't breathe.

CHANNELE: I don't know where to put myself. When you
look at me like this, it cuts me in two. (*Beat.*) What can I
give you?

SCHNECK: Your intelligence. Your beauty. Your love. I
was scared to say but now it's out. I feel better. You know
I can't get used to you. Every day you surprise me.
That's it.

CHANNELE: Oh, Schneck, you don't know what I have
seen. And now, what am I supposed to do with what you
just told me?

SCHNECK: Just love me.

CHANNELE: I don't know how.

SCHNECK: If we enter the war I'll go to Europe and fight.
Then you'd love me more. Huh?

CHANNELE: Rachel.

SCHNECK: What about Rachel?

CHANNELE: Nothing.

SCHNECK: You like me?

CHANNELE: Sure I like you.

SCHNECK: A little? A lot?

CHANNELE: How do you measure, silly. Sure, a lot. When
you get close like that I feel all hot inside, I don't know
where to put myself, your eyes all shiny for me.

SCHNECK: Tonight, when everyone is asleep. Can I come to you?

CHANNELE; My chest feels like there's a stone in it. And my eyes, like fragments of glass in them.

SCHNECK: Just to lie with you? That's all.

CHANNELE: I don't know. I just feel so much inside me. All those people. Gail, Rachel, Mother, all pounding inside my head. And now you, like this. My head will burst.

SCHNECK: I want us to be married.

ESTHER: It's snowing! It's like a postcard, gleaming sun on the white snow.

ANNIE: …and so cold.

ESTHER: You think we'll die in a Christmas card?

CHANNELE: Gail's dead.

ESTHER: What?

CHANNELE: Dead.

ESTHER: Gail?

CHANNELE: Dead.

ESTHER: (*Absently.*) In Moscow, after the Revolution they sang the Marseillaise before every performance.
(*She sings the first few bars of la Marseillaise gently.*)

CHANNELE: I saw the ambulance take her body wrapped in a white sheet. Her eyes wide open.

ESTHER: Rachel?

CHANNELE: Calm.

ESTHER: My little girl. My pretty Gail. All gone?

CHANNELE: Gone.

ESTHER: My babies. All my babies gone?

CHANNELE: Evie was gurgling in a police officer's arms as if nothing happened.

ESTHER: Oh, my Gittele. My angel girl.

CHANNELE: Gone now.

ESTHER: Oh, my pretty one. My darling, darling pretty one.

ANNIE: Esther. (*Puts a coat on her.*) It's cold.

ESTHER: Dance, Gittele, dance for your mummy, darling. That's it. What a pretty smile. Oh, my darling girl, how I love to see you dance and sing just like mommy did.

CHANNELE: I used to dance for you too, mommy.

66

ESTHER: (*Ignores CHANNELE.*) Don't cry, darling, it's
only new teeth coming, mommy will sing to you. (*Sings
'Maydele nit vayn'.*)

JOSEPH: Who will say kaddish?

ESTHER: Her little arms around my neck.

CHANNELE: Nobody...

ESTHER: I went to Bloomingdale's. Yes I did.

(*Light change as ESTHER goes into dream sequence.
FAYGELE has a sign which says BLOOMINGDALE'S.
Sound of cash register. Women's voices. A model, played by
GAIL, in a fur coat walks by with a price tag on the coat.
She is showing it in the hope that someone will buy it.*)

Shayn, so shayn. Look at that fur garment. Hundreds of
dollars and I don't have a cent to call my own. Is that
you Gittele? Is that yours? Gittele where did you get the
money for it? Oh the leather department. I need a new
purse. Excuse me Miss.

(*The saleswoman is played by RACHEL.*)

You remind me of someone. Oh look at this lovely
leather purse, oh the smell. Soft calf. I am sure I know
you? (*Looks down.*) Oh. There's a puddle on the floor.
Here in Bloomingdale's! Such dreck! Yellow. Verstinkene
piss. Someone pissed! Right here. In Bloomingdale's!
They should be ashamed. Why is everyone looking at
me?

(*The model in the fur coat and the saleswoman push ESTHER
away.*)

Why are you throwing me out? Me? I wuz a star.

(*Light change back to the present.
A WOMAN in a headscarf comes on.*)

WOMAN: Please, give something. For Shabbas.

(*A dog barks in the distance.*)

SCHNECK: That dog's got more in its belly than I have.

ESTHER: For Shabbas? You want nothing my girl, you'll
get nothing.

CHANNELE: I can't bear it. (*She runs offstage. Sound of
screeching breaks and car headlights. Car accelerates at speed.*)

SCHNECK: (*Running up to her.*) Channele!!! (*He comes
onstage with CHANNELE, who has been knocked down, in
his arms. He leaves her in ESTHER's lap.*)

ESTHER: 'In the cold cold ground.'

CHANNELE: (*Whispering.*) I'm here, mother, Channele.

ESTHER: Get away from me. You with your lies. Gittele.
Gently. Stop gnawing. (*Back to memory.*) So greedy.
Always so greedy. You'll eat me up. Such a pretty dolly.
The prettiest of all my babies. Your father was strong as
an ox. A god. He makes love like an army. Oh, you, you
are so greedy. Greedy Gittele.

CHANNELE: What about my father?

ESTHER: (*Pulls out some hair. Joseph picks it up.*) First my
teeth fall out and now my hair.
(*JOSEPH takes a notebook from his pocket and puts the hair
in the book.*)
What are you doing?

JOSEPH: Each hair of your head is precious to me.

ESTHER: Mother and father one flesh. 'They laid him in
the cold, cold ground.' Look Gittele, it's glistening
diamonds everywhere. (*She touches the ground.*) Poor
Joseph. I sold the diamond you gave me. Each diamond
will vanish into slush. Like us. (*She rocks CHANNELE in
her arms.*) Darling Gittele. We'll go to the mountains. I'll
show you France and Switzerland. Mountains are made
from land forced up into huge folds over millions of
years? (*Beat.*) Gittele, do you know that I love you?

CHANNELE: (*Sadly.*) I love you too mother. (*Beat.*)
Everything is rotten, isn't it?

SCHNECK: Esther. Channele's hurt

ESTHER: Look at the stars. They're so clear Gittele.

CHANNELE: Yes mother. That one it's dazzling green.

ESTHER: (*Brutally.*) The stars are long dead.

CHANNELE: Like us. The moon is bright. Is it dead too?

JOSEPH: She's a movie star in a shimmering lamé dress
waiting to be discovered.

CHANNELE: My feet are ice.

ESTHER: Let's go to the Plaza. We'll find a big room for
all of us. (*Lucid.*) What will happen to Rachel?

CHANNELE: They'll fry her.

ESTHER: And Eddie?

CHANNELE: Tucked up warm with Evie where the
    Brooklyn pollution's so thick they don't see the stars.
    You think there's a God up there who will protect us?
ESTHER: Ein schmetterling.
CHANNELE: A butterfly. That's all we are? I'm a butterfly,
    look at me!
ESTHER: Gittele, darling, we are in France. No the bad
    men are in France, we are not safe. Only in America can
    we be safe. Mommy will take care of you now.
CHANNELE: Please stop it. Oh the pain.
ESTHER: Only a few more minutes and then we'll drink
    chocolate. I'll order hot chocolate! Hurry, Gittele. We'll
    soon be there. Rachele. Channele. Hurry. All those
    people screaming and shouting, look the Statue of
    Liberty! (*Sings a few bars from the American National
    Anthem in Yiddish.*)
JOSEPH: Hold my hand, Esther.
ESTHER: I'm going to be a big star. A big American star!
    But you've got to be good little girls and do as mommy
    tells you.
    (*CHANNELE is dead.*)
    Wake up Gittele. Mommy will look after you. We'll soon
    be covered up in a nice warm bed with a full tummy and
    your little arms around me, Gittele come give mommy a
    kiss. Oh, I am so happy! (*She shivers.*) Why is it so cold
    Gittele. Cuddle up close. Oh darling. You are cold, oh so
    cold. (*She slumps.*)
ESTHER: (*Dying.*) Rudy ready? Ready Rudy.
    (*JOSEPH picks her up and dances with her body and as
    lights dim to blackout the tango music is played from the
    wedding scene.*)

The End.

English translation from Scene 13

MANKELE: You are so beautiful, Rivkele. Come to me. Put your hand on my breast.

RIVKELE: My father, he'll wake up.

MANKELE: No, Rivkele, your father won't know. Isn't it good, Rivkele? Isn't it good? Do you want to marry me?

RIVKELE: Yes, yes, Mankele. I do. I do.

MANKELE: Wait, wait, Rivkele, until your father and mother are asleep. Would you like to lie with me in a bed, Rivkele?

RIVKELE: Yes, yes, I will, I will.

Glossary of Yiddish words

Boychick – a term of affection for a boy

Clotz/nebbish/schmuck/shmo – fool

Dass mir nicht gefellt – deliberately bad German for 'that doesn't please me'

Gelt – money

Genug – enough

A glayzele Tay – a little glass of tea

Kishkes – guts

L'chaim – the traditional toast meaning 'to life' in Hebrew

Liebchen – little love

Meshuggah – crazy

Schlep – drag your own body or carry

Schlong – penis

Schmatters – old clothes or rags

Schmooze – engage in gossip or warm conversation

Schnorrer – beggar

Shabbes – Friday night to Saturday night; Jewish day of rest

Shine/schayn – beautiful or handsome

Stuffed helzel – traditional East European titbit; the neck of the chicken is stuffed with breadcrumbs, onions, chicken fat and herbs

Tochas – bottom

Verstinkene – stinking

Yentzer – fucker

WOMAN IN THE MOON

dedicated to Rudi Kennedy,
Yves Béon and Eugenia Rosenberg,
who was the original Dora
in the play

Characters

WERNHER VON BRAUN
DORA MAITLAND (née ROSENBERG)
a New York Times journalist
MISS AMERICA

The ensemble
FLAVIO
NIKOS
PIERRE
WOMAN AT THE PARIS OPERA
LITTLE GIRL BOMB VICTIM IN LONDON
FREDDIE
RUDI
IRENA
Dora's mother
THE SINGER
TWO BRITISH SOLDIERS
at the liberation of Belsen
RAF PILOT
KAPOS
GERMAN FIREMEN
FRENCH WORKERS SENT TO A BROTHEL

With doubling the original production used twelve actors. It can be staged minimally with four actors. The set was a scaffolding tower and a raised walkway with room underneath for people to crouch during the Belsen section.

Woman on the Moon was first performed at the Arcola Theatre on 13 March 2001, with the following cast:

VON BRAUN, Thomas Huber

DORA, Ruth Posner

MISS AMERICA, Rachel Gaffney Greetham

FLAVIO/NIKOS, Demetri Alexander

PIERRE, Ned Palmer

WOMAN AT THE OPERA, Adi Lerer

BOMB VICTIM, Lesley Lightfoot

FREDDIE, Ben Paterson

RUDI/PILOT, Gordon Kemp

IRENA, Anette Victoria Ness

THE SINGER, Phyn Nevelle

BRITISH SOLDIER, Carl Hargreaves

Director, Julia Pascal

Designer, Merav Weinstein

Movement direction, Thomas Kampe

Original music, Kyla Greenbaum

Lighting, Ian Watts

Sound, Colin Brown

Company Manager, Barbara Egervary

Scene 1

Prologue. Music: St Matthew's Passion.

The stage is full of people crossing at the same time. They are dressed in costumes ranging from the 1940s to the present day. They do not see one another. A man is on a mobile phone talking. A woman dressed in 1940s style is dragging a doll. The group disappears leaving a man dressed as a little boy with a toy rocket. He tries to make it fly.

Scene 2

Wernher VON BRAUN talks to God.

VON BRAUN: Please God. Let me make a rocket. And a rocket that flies to the moon. (*As God.*) Don't be silly. Nobody can fly to the moon. Only Gods. (*As Boy.*) But I want to. (*As God.*) You are not a God. (*As Boy.*) I will be good. (*As God.*) No. (*As Boy.*) I will do anything you want. (*As God.*) Anything I want? (*As Boy.*) I will eat all my greens. (*As God.*) That's nothing. (*As Boy.*) What can I do to go to the moon? (*As God.*) Always obey your elders. (*As Boy.*) That's easy. (*As God.*) Then you'll fly to the moon. (*As Boy.*) Is that all I have to do? Obey? (*As God.*) That's right. (*As Boy.*) Oh thank you God. Oh and God. (*As God.*) Yes child. (*As Boy.*) Do I have to pay to go to the moon? (*As God.*) Oh no. If you do what is asked of you, you will be paid in champagne. And you will fly up to the stars and never burn your wings.

Scene 3

Song. The Rise and Rise of Wernher VON BRAUN.

Oh yes sir.
He saw nothing.
Oh yes God.
He saw nothing. *Nichts niemals*
nothing ever.
As the crane takes the men up

And up and up. Up to the stars. Men, scarecrows hanging
high in the stars
What could be sweeter?
Than to die so high for a dream in the sky?
And you don't really mind. It's the moon you will find.
Nichts niemals.
Nothing never.
Way up past the swallow. Make a new tomorrow.
Von Braun watches through his office window. Necks
stretched up to heaven.
But no he sees nothing, for his touch. Only the moon
waiting for his touch, for his touch.

Scene 4

Daughters of America.

MISS AMERICA: Well. I am honoured to be allowed the
chance to speak before the Daughters of America. More
than honoured, I am thrilled, more than thrilled I am
flattered. But, even more than that, I want to say that I
am privileged to introduce you to one of the greatest
inventors of the century. This man, is a man who holds
the key to the universe. Now me. Little ol' me, what do I
know? (*Does a Donald Duck impersonation.*) That's the
extent of what I can do. Disney. But this man, this great
man is a visionary. He talks to presidents and prime
ministers, he speaks to scientists and technicians. He
even has dinner with our own President Kennedy! Ladies
it is my pleasure to introduce Mr Wernher von Braun.
(*Applause.*)

VON BRAUN: Thank you Miss America. You are a
charming and beautiful lady. And I am sure you have
many more achievements than you say.

MISS AMERICA: No before I won the crown of Miss
America, I was only a Rockette at New York's Radio
City Music Hall!

VON BRAUN: You are a Rockette and I make rockets!
How about that! (*Beat.*)

MISS AMERICA (*Laughs.*) And you know I first saw you
Mr von Braun? It was on your Disney TV show when I
was a teenager in the Fifties. You charmed the whole
nation and made all of America just crazy about space.
Mr Disney liked you very much and so did we. Wasn't it
called Tomorrowland?

VON BRAUN: That's right Miss America.

MISS AMERICA: And ladies if I am Miss America then
Mr von Braun is surely Mr America?

(*He laughs.*)

I remember rocket models and a spoke-wheeled
platform, I remember men just floating off into space.

VON BRAUN: It was so popular that I got called up all the
time with guys wanting to buy tickets to the moon. Had
to get my number removed from the telephone directory.
You see the moon is a magical place. Just look at that
sky. On a cold, clear night in the mountains you hear
nothing. Maybe a car passing somewhere in the distance.
And then there is silence so harsh it cracks your skull.
Look up. The black sky is naked. Except for a few
shimmering stars. Some are brighter than others. One
glimmers over you; a greenish sparkle. And you think
there is someone up there. Someone trying to
communicate. Not a Daughter of America but perhaps a
daughter of the moon? From her eyes, so many million
years away to yours. Look further, past those dimmer
stars. Hundreds. Maybe thousands. And there, over to
the right, a very bright one. A man is so small. He looks
up at all that distant life and wants to touch it. And the
man, he sees only an iota of what is on offer. Out there,
the thin crescent moon. You can almost reach out and
take it. When I was a boy I dreamt I would go to the
moon. I thought it was all snow with pine trees with
wolves and bears.

(*Music from St Matthew's Passion – Blut Nur.*)

In Peenemunde I used to look at the moon from this
magical place with islands and water everywhere. In this
Baltic wonderland there were fir trees and birch trees,
sandy earth and sea. The noise of wild birds was the only

sound in the whole world. I heard that the marvellous
wild geese of Peenemunde hibernated to the moon and I
saw myself riding on the back of a goose to a wondrous
place with waterfalls and lakes, wild tigers and strange
birds. I used to imagine I was the only little boy on earth
and that I would fly to the moon in a spaceship which I
had made . Dear ladies, you thought I was going to
mystify you with lunar technology and here I am
dreaming of my childhood. I know you don't want to
hear technical details so I will tell you quite simply. We,
on this earth, we only have one moon. The moon orbits
around the earth in twenty nine days, twelve hours and
forty four minutes. When you fly to the moon you weigh
a sixth of what you weigh on the earth. No more diets!
When you look at your horoscopes, you think of Mars as
the god of war. Did you also consider that Mars also has
one moon? Saturn has moons. So does Jupiter. Looking
out at the immensity to the great suns and circling
planets, can you accept that man must spend all his days
cooped up and crawling on the tiny surface of this earth?
Don't you believe that one day we will bridge the seas of
space? We must look to distant planets. We must travel.
We must adventure. I have designed a passenger ship
that can land on Mars's polar caps. A ship with skids.
Travellers will arrive with food and journey on to
warmer areas of Mars. Rather like going to a seaside
holiday. It's easy.
(*Sound: 'Once Upon A Time In The West'.*)
Europeans thought America just as impossible. Then
they came to the East Coast and gradually, on
wagontrains, through hardship and despite terrible
conditions, Americans gradually won the West. And now
we need new frontiers. We have conquered the world and
we have to conquer the moon! First the moon and then
Mars. How will we live on Mars? First of all, men will
travel there in a rocket, set up fuel stations and then dig
underground tunnels which will be air-conditioned. They
will stabilise the environment for tourists. This, no

doubt, you find unbelievable. But first, like Leonardo da Vinci, we have to dream. After the dream comes the reality. Just imagine if Colombus had never dreamed of America?

(*Applause.*)

MISS AMERICA: Marvellous, just marvellous. We are all ready to take the first spaceship to Mars if you will be our guide.

VON BRAUN: Well, thank you but this may be a little premature. We will have to get to the moon first.

MISS AMERICA: Champagne? From France specially for you Mr von Braun.

Scene 5

Champagne. Sound of champagne cork popping. Sound of rocket going up. Light change. Flashback.

VON BRAUN: It landed!!! London. Wonderful. Champagne. For everyone. This is a good one – Moet and Chandon. Worth every pfennig.

(*Holding up a glass.*)

Champagne bubbles must explode very lightly. And consistently. The liquid is at its best when it is a pale yellow. Luminous. Consistent. Always consistent. One tiny explosion after another, delicately balanced, a kinetic work of art, no beginning, no end, like the world. God made infinite bubbles bubbling on my tongue, tiny little bangs on my palate, tickling my nose, my lips, deliciously champagning their way down the tube that is my throat to the bag that is my stomach and exploding lightly against the stomach wall, tickling me inside and outside. Prost. Good health to us and hello London! Welcome to my new rocket. Her name is V for Vengeance. Beats the Spitfire our champagne rocket, don't you think, Mr Churchill? Your good health!

Interlude

Song of the V2 Victim.

CHILD: (*Sitting up in bed.*)
And oh, I heard nothing. Not a bird. Not a scream.
Not a din.
And then the walls came folding in. With a bang.
With a roar
With a crash. Plaster and everything red coming towards
me. Asleep in the bed
Mummy tuck me in! Day becomes night. In sunshine so
bright.
Why did the plane make no sound? Our house is a
mound.
Mummy cannot be found.
Her head smashed on the ground.

Scene 6

The Intruder.

MISS AMERICA: Another glass of champagne Mr von
Braun?
VON BRAUN: Thank you.
DORA: Maitland. From the *New York Times.* May I have a
word?
VON BRAUN: *New York Times.* Well of course
DORA: The Daughters of America seemed to appreciate you.
VON BRAUN: Ah the American ladies.
DORA: You are their champion.
VON BRAUN: Not yet. Perhaps one day.
DORA: Oh you are being modest. I would say you are their
hero now.
VON BRAUN: If we get to the moon.
DORA: Yes. The moon. (*Beat.*) The English say it is made
of green cheese. And the English talk of the Man In The
Moon. A romantic people. Like the Germans.
VON BRAUN: So I hear. To my regret I have never been to
England.

DORA: No?

VON BRAUN: No.

DORA: But you sent them a few messages.

VON BRAUN: I beg your pardon?

DORA: In a rocket or two.

VON BRAUN: Oh, my dear Miss…?

DORA: Maitland.

VON BRAUN: That was war.

DORA: Indeed.

VON BRAUN: You said the New York Times?

DORA: That's right.

VON BRAUN: A good newspaper.

DORA: Yes.

VON BRAUN: What sort of article are you writing?

DORA: Operation Paperclip.

VON BRAUN: Curious name I always thought.

DORA: Nazi scientists to the US.

VON BRAUN: Where are you from Miss Maitland?

DORA: I am a US citizen. (*Beat.*) Like you.

VON BRAUN: Your accent.

DORA: Do I have an accent?

VON BRAUN: Everyone has an accent.

DORA: Lower East Side.

VON BRAUN: I would say Poland.

DORA: You have a good ear.

VON BRAUN: Your war. How was it?

DORA: That's what I was going to ask you.

VON BRAUN: What's your real name?

DORA: Dora.

VON BRAUN: Dora?

DORA: The name means something to you?

VON BRAUN: Oh I once knew a Dora.

(*Flashback.*)

DORA: My name is not Dora Rosenberg it is Anna
Kosieck.

VON BRAUN: You were not in Dora?

DORA: No. I was hiding in the earth.

(*Flashback.*)

81

Scene 7

DORA in hiding.

DORA: It's all to do with smells and sounds. Lice have a certain smell. When you see them moving under wallpaper they have a certain sweetish smell. My hair stands on end to watch them moving. Under blankets. Just me and three women and some pillows. Over our heads, in the dug out, are rabbits. Then, there is where we are, with newspapers on the walls. And lice crawling under the newspapers. I don't know what the newspapers say. I am two and a half and I am walking. My arms full of toys. Very tired.

IRENA: If you are too tired drop the toys.

DORA: No. She is a German doll with a soft grey beige body. Her face is sewn on papier mâché card with glossy paint eyelashes. The shelter, you climb down with a stepladder. And inside the room is as high as a table. The women have to crouch. Not me. I sleep between them. A sheet over us all. Cold. Their bodies higher than mine and the space is cold. All day they sew and make jumpers. They are knitting and I hold the wool my hands like two soldiers. No noise. Mother makes me a doll and, at night, the rat comes to eat the head off. But I say no. And we fight. He gets the head Three women. Mother. Sister-in-law. Niece. While they sew I talk to my doll. They talk and laugh and I know their laughs are about men and women. And what they do. They laugh and I laugh too. They see that I laugh and they laugh even more. Mother says, 'no, go to sleep you mustn't listen to that.' Sometimes mother is not there. She goes up the stepladder and disappears. When she comes back she says, someone has to take me in for a couple of weeks until the danger goes. I go to a woman in the country.
(*The group come onstage with a bed.*
A WOMAN gets on the bed with her SS boyfriend.)

WOMAN: My boyfriend is in the SS. Get under the bed. Hide and never make a sound.

DORA: Under the bed it is dusty.

(*The couple copulate.*)

My name is not Dora Rosenberg it is Anna Kosiek. Anna Kosiek. Anna Kosiek. Mother!!!!

Scene 8

IRENA walks.

IRENA: I have to get out into the air.

(*The group walk as people in the street.*)

Walk. Spazieren. Maszerovac. I walk. You walk. He walks. There is someone walking behind me. He walks. Who is he? Does he recognise me? From the Warsaw days? When there was no ghetto. Perhaps his sister had a dress made in my shop? He's not so close now. I walk. Silence. A car. Slow. Coming closer. My heart will smash. Look ahead. Don't turn round. It's coming close. He is singing with the window wound down.

(*Hatikvah is sung.*)

From my youth. Hatikvah. Hope. Only a Jew would sing that. Only a Jew would know that. Only a Jew would turn around. I walk. I walk. I walk. I don't turn round. Jewish scum. Out to catch a Jew for his Nazi paymasters. He's getting closer the filthy Jewcatcher. Turn now and I will be a pillar of ash. He is next to me now. Singing softly. I walk. I walk. I walk. The song means nothing to me. I hear nothing. I am an Aryan. How many did he catch today? Hope! How much longer must I walk and my feet are dead? I want to sit in a warm café and drink something hot. I want to sit in a restaurant wearing a fur coat not trawl in worker's clothes like a kitchen maid. I walk. I walk. He walks. Again. That man is following. The first one from before Hope. I walk. He walks. I stop. He stops. He knows me. My face hasn't changed even after all I have seen. I walk and if I run, he is stronger, he will catch me. 'Jew' he will yell like so many I have seen suddenly screaming Jew in the street. Jew 'he'll' yell and I will freeze like a rabbit. What will happen to my baby? Who will care for her if he yells 'Jew'. I walk. I stop. I turn. The man is looking at me. I look. He looks. He looks down. I look down. In his hand there is something red. Something strange and stiff. I want to laugh. I want to empty my lungs and laugh with relief. Is that all! Thank God.

DORA: Back under the rabbits once comes mother with chicken. Her hands are wet with the fat of the chicken. I watch the fat. I rub her hands.

IRENA I am not a Jew. I am blonde. And tall. I speak perfect German. I am the wife of a German officer.

DORA: (*Underground.*) Bang. The boots are marching nearby. Marching so loud the ceiling is falling in and the rabbits will fall on top of us. Mother and the other women are holding up the ceiling. (*Screams.*) I am frightened.

(*Flashforward. Return to today.*)

DORA: Is it correct that you were in the SS?

VON BRAUN: Where did you hear that?

DORA: There are files.

VON BRAUN: Really?

DORA: That you joined the Nazi Party in 1937.

VON BRAUN: You have been busy.

DORA: Very early that. Thirty seven.

VON BRAUN: I was a scientist.

DORA: Yes? From an aristocratic family. What did they feel about you joining the SS in 1940? Proud?

VON BRAUN: It was a technicality. You like science?

DORA: Very much. Let's get back to your V rockets.

VON BRAUN: Now the V1. It's nothing special. Can't depend on it. Not very efficient. Not very fast. The RAF can knock it out easily – kaput. But the V2, well she is quite a different baby. High she goes, higher almost to the moon and then down she goes, faster than the speed of sound. The V1 and the V2 landed on the wrong planet. They were meant for the moon and Mars. I never planned them for England. The Soviets got to space first but we Americans will be the first on the moon. We will have satellites.

(*Stage right MAN with two mobile phones one to each ear.
One is giving information which he relays to the other.*)

PLAINCLOTHES POLICEMAN: London. Chancery
Lane. I am following a black Renault truck with five
men and one woman. They just robbed Lloyds Bank on
the Strand. Follow them up High Holborn.

VON BRAUN: We will be able to detect someone robbing a
bank from a satellite in space and then we beam back the
information to the police. Ultimate surveillance. Think
of it all crime all over the world will be punished

DORA: All crimes?

VON BRAUN: Think of it a world without crime!

(*The stage fills with men in striped pyjamas working. Sound
of plane in the distance. They look up hopefully. Sound of the
interior of a Lancaster.*)

Scene 9

The RAF Man.

MAN IN RAF UNIFORM: (*He is a map reader in a plane.*)
Dark August night. I sit in the black. Straight ahead.
Now to the right. You see a railway line. Follow the track
as it curves round to the left. And past the lake. Pick up
the track again. There is a wood. Follow the wood. On
and on past the trees and the birds. On and on past the
wolves and the wildcats. And the witches riding to
heaven. Dreaming. Am I dreaming? Right! Surprise.
This one is going to be a big surprise. That's what they
told me back at base. I don't know. I have no idea what
the target is. I give the instructions. I tell you all. I am
the voice that is behind the hand, that lifts the lever and
yes! Let her go! Let them go! Give it to them, whatever
the target is go! Now!!! Home James. Home we go. And
then they can tell us what we bombed. We got Jerry full
in the face.

VON BRAUN: Wrong. They thought they'd wiped us out
and all they did was kill a few slave workers. We had to
find somewhere secret.

DORA: A slave factory?

VON BRAUN: If you like to put it that way.

DORA: A pact with the devil?

VON BRAUN: No. Not the devil.

Scene 10

Tourism in Dora.

The company line up in striped uniforms.

VON BRAUN: And welcome to Dora! Lovely name don't you think. Dora. Adore 'er. Don't you just? Dora. Greek isn't it? Gift of the Gods. Fancy. Lovely situation. In the Harz mountains. Harz that means tree sap in German. Another lovely name. Romantic. Goethe. Schiller? *Du bist nur ein trüber Gast auf dieser Erde?* After the British bomb my Baltic wonderland in Peenemunde we find somewhere really impenetrable. A place called Dora. There is nothing there. Apart from the mountain So we build a tunnel. Just like rabbits. Well, we find men to do that for us. There are strong young men to be found from Auschwitz, from Buchenwald. First they do it with their bare hands. Later, when there's a bit of a tunnel there are the drills. All day and all night. We have to move quickly. I have to persuade Hitler of the importance of the new weapons. It has to be cheap. The SS take the men and rent them out to Volkswagen. The SS is a business. It must make a good profit from the men in Dora. Twelve, fifteen hours a day they work with only a half hour lunch break but, of course, no lunch. Volkswagen. The people's car. Volkswagen doing all that fine work to make my rockets fly. Oh Dora. You are my gift from the gods.

Scene 11

Babel.

Actors stand in a line and one after another say a line from the play in French, German, Italian, Russian, Polish or any other language that can be found in Auschwitz. The last person to speak is NIKOS who speaks Greek.

Scene 12

A lost Greek.

NIKOS: And all these languages. And where are the other Greeks? And where is my brother Spiro? I lost them somewhere when the Germans came to round us up. But I am not even a Jew. I told them but they wouldn't believe me. They say the Inquisition threw us out of Spain in 1492 so, even if it is true, that's a long time ago and the Jew has worn off me. 1492 and now it's 1942. Same numbers. Different way round. Same story. Why did they put me in the train with all the Jews? I am not a Jew. I told them and told them. I have no religion. I am an atheist. They pulled my trousers down, looked between my legs, then they took me away. 1492. 1942. Funny how just being born in the wrong sequence of numbers can make such a difference. Unlucky that one nine four two combination. Suppose it is just a question of numbers and whether they cut the skin from you or not. After Poland. What will happen? Do you think we will go on to Spain? In school, I learnt that in Toledo there are paintings by El Greco. And that he had a Jewish mistress. They lived together in the Jewish quarter of Toledo. El Greco. The Greek. I want to speak Greek again. Does anybody here speak Greek?

Interlude

Song of the Triangle.

The singer points to the prisoners and they move off to prepare for the next scene during the song. By the end of the song they are lying on the floor.

> The triangle is for your short life
> You with the knife
> Black for the criminal
> Best hope your pain is minimal
> Red for the communist
> You we have on our list
> Enemy of the state
> Tomorrow comes too late.

Scene 13

The Corpse Game.

FREDDIE: You like it here in Dora? You want to keep fit? Try the latest corpse game? You want to learn how? I'll tell you. First you watch a male nurse. He takes a fresh corpse, let's call him Monsieur, fresh from the infirmary. First the nurse has to do his job. That is please his masters by writing monsieur's number on his stomach. Then he takes monsieur to the showers, washes him, brings him back and the game begins. I have to say the game is very economical because all you need, apart from the corpse, and there are plenty of them, is a second male nurse and a wheelbarrow. Now the exercise goes like this. One man takes monsieur's arms and the other takes his legs. Monsieur has to be beautifully balanced because the body has to neatly arrive on the stretcher. A dead man weighs between five and six stone. Perfect. Not too much so no-one gets tired and not too little so as to make things too easy. Ah you think the game is easy? But let me tell you there are problems. Sometimes the nurses miss. Sometimes Monsieur falls in the wrong place or else he lands sideways on the stretcher. Monsieur, in fact, becomes a kind of ball. He has to land just so. But Monsieur can have a tough time. First his nose breaks. Then the arms dislocate. But monsieur is very considerate. Monsieur does not bleed. It's just when he starts to fall apart well then the game gets really tough.

(*Movement sequence. Cast lie on their backs and laugh hysterically giving the appearance of grotesque laughing corpses. They stop laughing and begin twitching as one inmate walks through the scene and breaks it.*)

Scene 14

A Visit to the Brothel.

ONE: 'Good news,' he said. 'You French prisoners. You're not going to the tunnel.'

TWO: What? A hanging?

ONE: The SS is organising a little entertainment, And guess what it is?

TWO: I don't want to know.

ONE: A brothel!!!!

TWO: A brothel?

ONE: Here in Dora. With real prostitutes.

TWO: I don't believe you.

ONE: You're going to a brothel. That's what they said.

TWO: I have been working eighteen hours. I just want to sleep.

VON BRAUN: *Hosen runter.*

THREE: Trousers down.

ONE: Oh God.

TWO: Oh God.

VON BRAUN: Over there. That hut. Girls are waiting.

ONE: Oh God.

VON BRAUN: Trousers down.

(*Men lower their trousers. Backs to the audience.*)

THREE: Go inside.

ONE: I can't do that. Did you ever see a corpse fuck a woman?

TWO: Oh God look at her. She has all her hair. Look at her all powder and paint. Oh the shame of it. Oh God, what will she think of me?

THREE: Stop!!

ONE: Stop? I can't even start.

TWO: Me neither.

VON BRAUN: The water's off.

TWO: When was it on?

VON BRAUN: Hygiene regulations.

ONE: I'm full of fleas and filth and he tells me the water's not working.

TWO: That's alright then.

ONE: Back we go.

Scene 15

A Night at the Opera.

Gluck's 'Orpheus & Eurydice'. During her monologue he goes to her and they dance.

MAN IN THE BROTHEL LINE UP: I used to go to the Palais Garnier with my wife. She would comb her hair and put it up into a chignon.

WOMAN: I remember our walking up the steps and seeing the marble staircase do you remember my darling? Up and up we went into that wonderful room with the mirrors everywhere. Remember that sound of the man on the stairs. 'Programme! Programme!' We queued all night for the cheapest tickets. Remember how we took it in turns to buy coffee not to feel the cold. Then we would rush home and snuggle under the blankets and make love though our limbs ached with standing or sitting on the cold paving stones. Then, when you went to get the coffee, there would always be some man who would try and pick me up. Oh my darling it's so long since we held each other. Oh my darling. When will I see you again? Will this war ever end? Oh and I forgot. Do you remember the glass of champagne we bought in the interval? One glass between us. And how we tasted that champagne. And how we loved the sumptuous dresses even though our own clothes were quite modest. And now, those modest clothes, seem to me like the greatest riches. But the greatest wealth I can imagine is to touch your skin and stroke your hair, to feel your arms and to have your weight on my body. Oh my darling we will soon sing and dance together to our old gramophone, we will go to bars and drink Pernod. Oh my darling this war will soon be over and we will once again hold hands in the opera – so near to the gods

Scene 16

Italian Opera.

Starts with a movement scene to Mozart's 'The Marriage of Figaro' (Cherubino's 'Voi che sapete che cosa e amor'). As this plays VON BRAUN stands in front of the ensemble who line up before him. He waves them to the right or to the left as a Selection for the gas chamber. As he leaves the Selection, the ensemble makes a group and Flavio stands in front of them.

FLAVIO: I am Flavio. One of the jobs is to cart the material from the main site to the tunnel. It might be anything. Fibre glass. Liquid oxygen tanks. Sheet iron. Metal work. I am an Italian prisoner of war. The Russians hate me, they let sharp instruments drop in my way. They can't forgive me for the Italian divisions on the Soviet front. They know I'm Italian because of my khaki tatters and my pathetic, feathered hat. Italian chic. Shit. The iron sheet slips and cuts the tatters through. Cuts me right through. Why am I pissing in my pants? Only it's not piss. It's blood. Hey you hospital scum. You hack so-called doctors. What's that you are sewing me with? For God's sake give me something to take away the pain. Oh God I am going to scream. No I mustn't. 'Screaming Iti. Cowardly little wop', that's what they'll say. Oh God he sews me like he's laying bricks. His hands all filth inside me. (*Sings Mozart opera in Italian.*) I am going to faint. Please no. Not that. (*Sings louder. Laughter from the group.*) Let them laugh. And there in the bed next to me, that shit of a Czech. 'Italiano! Spaghetti! Spaghetti! Spaghetti!' Is that all he can think of to say? I don't give a shit. Let him shout 'spaghetti'! If only someone else spoke Italian here. And now the surgeons are coming with food. *Immer fressen mein lieber Mann?* I can't eat. My wound has a terrible smell. I have fever. Gangrene.

Scene 17

The Song of Survival.

The SINGER points to the company and sends them away during the song.

THE SINGER: Don't be too tall
    They'll pick you out
    Knock you about
    Don't be too small
    They'll pick you off
    Don't be too fat
    No chance of that
    You need a physique
    If you are going to peak
    Don't be too smart
    You'll be on a cart
    Of stiffs for paradise
    Oh you can tell who's who
    Russkie's feet are ten to two
    Yellow skin is Russkie too
    If there's flesh then
    Slave is new

    Talking with the hands
    Italians
    Czechs have a superior air
    They are never vulgaire

Poles hate the rest
Think they are the best
Even the Polish French
know Pole is not a mensch

And the Pole hates the Yid
And wants them all got rid
Hey Frenchy pussy licker
Minette
Look at the great French lovers
In their clown rags all in shit.

Scene 18

The Road from Auschwitz to Dora.

Sound of gypsy violin.

VON BRAUN: There was music in Dora. At night after
eighteen hours work, the gypsies, they played their
instruments or on a dish, a piece of wood, anything just
to have their own music. At night the men slept in the
barracks altogether.

FREDDIE: Must piss. Can't piss. Hold it. Sleep. Sleep. Him
next to me coughing. And him next to me swearing in
his sleep. And him almost on top of me sweating with
fear, his rags soak me through. Must piss. No hold it in.
Don't go. If you do you'll lose your sleep-place. Oh God
I am going to burst. Oh God I am going to piss all over.
No choice. Up and out. Past the hundreds of half-
sleeping groaners shaking with cold on the concrete
floor. Shaking with the cold I walk past the half-corpses.
Please God don't let the piss churn be full. Please God
don't let it be me who has to take it to be emptied. I
walk. To the piss churn. The churn awaits me. I stand. I
piss. Oh God the relief. Oh God it's full. Oh God I have
to lift it. No I won't take it. If I do, the piss will drench
me all over. The piss of so many men. All mixed
together. Someone walks nearby. It is another pissing
half-corpse. It's full.

ANDRZEJ: Come with me. We'll empty it.

FREDDIE: No.

ANDRZEJ: Do it or I'll get you.

FREDDIE: He has come to piss, that means that he has lost his sleep-place and I can take his.

ANDRZEJ: I said empty it

FREDDIE: No. I notice he is a Pole. They come for me later.

ANDRZEJ: We'll teach you to call us Poles shits.

FREDDIE: They whack me. My hips will break. My skin is a furnace. I see the man at the piss-churn telling the Poles, lying to the Poles about me. And then it is over. All this. Just for a piss.

(*Cast walk again during the gypsy music. A man emerges from the group.*)

DORA: Who is this man?

VON BRAUN: I don't know.

DORA: Who are you?

RUDI: Rudi, I am standing there in the line in Auschwitz. (*As if answering a question.*) Fifteen.

VOICE: Say you are eighteen.

RUDI: I am eighteen and I love working. (*As if answering a question.*) The bus or walk? Walk of course. Mother and sister. To the left. Cold. I am cold without my clothes. At least leave me my shoes. Cold. In the shower. My father. Doesn't want to go. I've never seen my father naked. While we shower my mother and sister are gassed. Run. Naked. Wet. Barefoot. Six of us in one bed in the block. Next morning. Tattooing. Ow it hurts. Like knitting needles. I am small. Someone gives me a very large suit. Clogs. Don't fit. Can't walk. Must walk. To the IG Farben factory. To build a road. I get an axe to break the clumps of earth before the cementing.

GUARD: You'll see your maker very soon kid. Road to Paradise. Himmelfahrt.

VON BRAUN: I wasn't in Auschwitz.

MAN: (*Shouting.*) Rudi! Stay alive.

RUDI: I never see father again.

VON BRAUN: I knew nothing.

(*Sound of bombing. The group look up.*)

GUARD: This is Dora not a holiday camp. Get the heavy stuff inside the tunnel.

MAN: British!

(*RUDI has material in his hand, he lets it fall.*)

RUDI: Shit I dropped it. I fall over a cable. He hits me with a piece of wood. There's a nail in it. It goes septic. I piss. Please pour the piss on my wound.

(*Nobody responds. WERNHER VON BRAUN walks past him.*)

GUARD: Don't look. (*Hits him.*)

RUDI: That's Wernher von Braun isn't it?

GUARD: (*Hits him.*) I told you.

VON BRAUN: Dora. Oh yes I was there.

Song of the Triangle (*continued*).

> White for the deserter
> You will go no further
> Cowards all will die
> None will hear your cry
> Black for the deviant
> We punish the miscreant
> Mischief is your rôle
> For us you have no soul.
>
> Pink for the queer
> To us you are not dear
> Fit for less than life
> Death is the sweetest knife.
>
> The Yid is yellow starred
> The bottom of the pile
> Dance and make us smile
> Before you all get charred.

GERMAN FIREMAN: Hey you. Come with us firemen. You are a lovely boy.

(*They caress him.*)

You are with us now. We will look after you. (*Beat.*) Oh God, you've got lice.

(*The group throw him aside. Sound of explosion.*)

SLAVE WORKER: Russians or Americans? Run Rudi. Run.

(*Sound of dogs.*)

RUDI: Help me. Oh please.

(*He runs into a group of men. Sound of explosion.*)

The Russians are coming.

Scene 19

The Train to Nowhere.

RUDI: Three days the SS make us march. We sleep in a freezing hut with only our dead comrades as our blankets.

VOICE: Get into those coal wagons.

(*Sound of train moving slowly.*)

RUDI: Oh God they are so open with the snow coming down on us.

(*The men scratch.*)

VOICE: Stop scratching or I'll shoot.

(*Sound of whistle, puff of steam locomotive starts up. Convoy on the move.*)

FREDDIE: Tourism in 1945 is not so bad. You are never lonely on a German train. Well-chaperoned, I'd say! I am one of fifty, not counting the SS guard. He takes a quarter of the space. Well he'd need to. He's got thick bones, muscles, fat. We, fifty skeletons, why should we need space? He also needs the room for his dogs. They love dogs the SS. That's why they feed them so much in front us who have eaten nothing since I don't know when. The problem is knowing how long we have been on this train from Dora to nowhere. I try to sleep and in the morning, those who were living are dead but we can't throw them over to make more room because there must always be fifty in the open car. They like even numbers the SS. Oh and now we stop. Well the SS must have his lunch. Potted meat. Bread. An apple. Some cheese. Can't have them missing their vitamins. And we go. And we stop. You see the problem. What to do with us. Here's a pretty little town. Hello Herr Burgermeister. Can we just stop the train and let off these thousands of filthy louse-ridden prisoners? (*Parodies the Mayor's reaction.*) Of course. My townspeople will love them. They will take them into their homes, wash and feed them and treat them with love and respect. Take the filthy pieces of shit out of my town. They wouldn't be here if the Jews and Communists hadn't started this stinking war. It's all their fault and if these skeleton scarecrows come near us then we'll just get out our shotguns and finish them off. Or let the kids just throw stones. That's all it will take to knock them from life. But then what do we do with the bodies? No for God's sake take those heaving heaps of filthy flesh out of our town. (*Stops playing the Mayor.*) It's cold. The SS guard clubs us to keep warm. No food but at least we get warmer. He clubs. More die. The dead insulate the cold from the hardly-living. Bodies make cushions. Where are the Yanks? Or the Russians? The SS man is tired from the clubbing and he sleeps with the rocking of the train. Birds sing. Kids look at the train of corpses and throw stones at us. Two half corpses make a run from the car to the grassy slope. They run in their heads but their legs have no calories. They slide down like young kittens trying to climb trees. Lazily the SS leaves the train to follow them and in a flash the men's heads explode all over the grass. We collect the bodies and bring them back into our rail car while the children clap wildly. The SS want the bodies back in the wagons. Fifty bodies set off and 50 bodies must arrive.

RUDI: Hey Dora you came with us. Dora lice. Dora in our bloody stinking lungs.

(*Train stops.*)

Belsen. Still no food.

Scene 20

Belsen.

MAN: There, on the other side of the barbed wire, a turnip
field.

RUDI: A tree.

(*He runs. RUDI taking out a bit of the bark of a tree from his
mouth. Sound of a tank arriving.*)

FIRST SOLDIER: Oh Jeesus. Oh Jeesus Christ. Look at the
bleedin' corpse walking up to me. If this is Belsen I want
to go home.

SECOND SOLDIER: There is a skeleton eating the bark of
a tree. (*He lifts corpses.*) Tree. Beech or oak? The United
States has about seven hundred and eighty-five species of
trees. Eve took an apple from a tree but what sort of tree
was that? That man is he eating ash or elm? There is the
copper purple beech and the blue or water beech. Oak is
the largest group in the beech family and there are four
hundred species of-oh God the stench. Coniferous,
deciduous. I am sitting in the school room in London
with a leaf in my hand. We will paint it in our art class
and Miss Wright, who is really quite fat says, 'Look at
the veins under the leaf, look it's like a skeleton.' Why is
that dead man walking towards me with tree in his
mouth? Cypress. Fir tree. Aspen, poplar goes all the way
to heaven like Jacob's ladder. Walking towards me slow
motion. Jesus don't let him touch me. Christ almighty
please don't let him touch me.

FIRST SOLDIER: Look over there. Those well-fed guys.
Tattooing themselves.

RUDI: Those are the guards. They are pretending to be
prisoners. Afraid of being punished.

Scene 21

The Interview.

VON BRAUN: Punished. Why? I did nothing.

DORA: I believe you.

VON BRAUN: That's right.

DORA: Your office. In Dora. It looked out onto the yard.

VON BRAUN: True.

DORA: Glass windows.

VON BRAUN: I saw the prisoners.

DORA: Yes.

VON BRAUN: I pitied them.

DORA: Did you.

VON BRAUN: What could I do?

DORA: You went to select prisoners.

VON BRAUN: We needed men.

DORA: You went to Buchenwald to pick out more French technicians for Dora.

VON BRAUN: That's right.

DORA: You knew their conditions.

VON BRAUN: It wasn't my business.

DORA: You saw.

VON BRAUN: I felt sorry for them.

DORA: And you never made a move to get them more food?

VON BRAUN: They were… (*Stops himself.*)

DORA: Yes?

VON BRAUN: Slaves. What could I do?

DORA: Slaves are bought and sold. They were worse than slaves.

VON BRAUN: Yes. It was war. Terrible things happened. I understand you.

DORA: But you were in the SS?

VON BRAUN: I hated all those costumes and carnival. It was so vulgar. I never even wore my SS uniform. Look, Hitler was the Führer: I wanted to build my rockets – it was just bad luck that all my work was linked to war. Rotten timing. You must realise, I was never anti-Semitic. All that propaganda just sickened me.

DORA: Not enough to make you do something?

VON BRAUN: What could I do?

DORA: You could have left the country.

VON BRAUN: I was a German scientists. I loved my country.

DORA: The United States welcomed German scientists.

VON BRAUN: I was not a traitor.

DORA: But you ran to the Americans in 1945.

VON BRAUN: That was different. My work, I couldn't afford that it might get lost.

DORA: So why in '45 and not '39?

VON BRAUN: In '39 there was so much to do. In '45 there was nothing left. What was my choice? The Yanks or the Communists. Nobody in their right mind would go to the Communists.

DORA: And if you had stayed in Germany?

VON BRAUN: Who knows.

DORA: You know very well.

VON BRAUN: What are you getting at? Spit it out.

DORA: Nuremberg. You would have been tried. That's what you couldn't risk. Twenty-seven thousand died in Dora. That's why you rushed to the American military.

VON BRAUN: And what did I have to hide?

DORA: We know you saw the hangings

VON BRAUN: Saboteurs. They would piss on the machinery parts or throw sand into the joints. They wanted to destroy my work

(*PIERRE sits at VON BRAUN's feet.*)

PIERRE At night I hear the sound of singing in Russian. Ah the Russians. I lie in my filthy cot, my filthy, louse-ridden blanket on my freezing wet carcass. Holding it tightly with my left hand and in my right hand, my half ration of sawdust bread from the morning for the rat gnawing at my gut. Half-dreaming, half-scratching, half-shifting; something moves above my head, tries to steal my saved crumbs. With both hands I leap to grab him but he's gone quicker than my breath with my filthy cover in his hands. Ah the Russian bed trick. Nobody escapes it except fellow Russkies. They stick together. Not like us Frenchmen. They stick together so that even the kapos are frightened to be alone with them. Even the thickest Ukrainian peasant here has protection from his brothers. An illiterate who can barely count can look to a Moscow – educated student because here they are all

Russkies. We, we look out for ourselves. If another
Frenchman or Hungarian is in trouble then we look
away. Ah the Russkies. Now, on this freezing morning
when the Americans should be here to save us, the SS
make us stand in the January snow and watch nine brave
Russians who made a run for it, they make us watch as the
rope is tied around their necks The Russians don't move.
The SS waits for the order of the Obersturmführer. The
waiting lasts an eternity. My eyes are sand but I can't
touch them. Slowly, very slowly they hang the rope to
the iron girder attached to the crane made to lift the
rockets. Now the crane will lift the men. The steel girder
has nine ropes around nine breathing necks. The nine
men go up. We close our eyes. The guard yells Schau!
Look! The bodies are hoisted up. They are standing on
tiptoe, faces stretched in agony, their eyes bulging.
(*Beat.*) And then it is over. Nine warm, breathing men
into nine puppets.
(*MEN come onstage. VON BRAUN ties a tie around their
necks and pins a faded carnation on their jackets during the
song and the dialogue.*)
THE SINGER: (*Singing.*) To remind us of our home.
  Makes us feel so alone
  A dinner we'll never have
  A wife we'll never see
  Angelique
  Marcelle
  Lulu
  A terrible thing to do.
MAN: Look. There's a Christmas tree!
MAN: In the middle of Dora. With coloured angels. And
  silver stars not yellow ones.
MAN: You think God is here?
MAN: God's on holiday. The other fella's taken his place.
MAN The Lord is my shepherd. I shall want. Yea though I
  walk through the valley of death he is not with me.
VON BRAUN: (*To the men in his nightmare.*) Leave me alone.
  The war is over.

Scene 22

War ends.

Bombing. Everyone freezes. It stops. Silence. People change clothes. It is the end of the war. Women come on in black evening dresses. They dance with empty arms. The men in striped pyjamas also dance grotesquely with nobody in their arms.

DORA: The war is over. I am big now. Four and a half.
They put me on a chair and I fall off. I have never been so far from the floor. Chopin Street. A big flat. So big I get lost. I sleep on the floor. A bed is too high. Under a pink duvet on the stone floor.
(*She climbs into a cupboard.*
Russian singing.
The men dance with the women and drink.)
They kiss me vodka kisses. They come from the embassy. Alone. I hate it. She is out with Russians and I all alone in the big flat. She leaves me supper. Polish white cheese and the cheese gets very salty because of my tears. I run out to Chopin Park. I am sick under every tree. They take me to a play called Father Comes Back. Poland is full of Father Comes Back. Stick men like marionettes. Mother has a new man in her bed every night. Mr Freeman takes me out to the cake shop. He buys me a Napoleon cake. He takes me to the fairground. I am sick. They come back together one day and say, we are married. I will not cry. They put a knife inside me but I will not cry. She has a new grey dress with loose pockets. Embroidery, red and blue, half sleeves. The skirt is cut on the cross. She wears high heels and has what people call a good figure. It is summer. A blonde summer bride. What happens if father comes back? I sleep under the table in the hall so that if he comes back in the night I can distract him. He mustn't find out that mother has a new husband. All night I wait crunching sour russet apples to keep myself

ready for when the door opens. Everyone is coming back. Skeletons on wheelbarrows. I must be ready. A man comes out of the wardrobe Daddy!!!

Scene 23

Back in the USA.

VON BRAUN: So you are not an American at all.

DORA: I am now. Like you

VON BRAUN: What is your religion Miss Maitland?

DORA: I am an atheist.

VON BRAUN: That's not what I mean.

DORA: I am a Jew.

VON BRAUN: My religion is rockets I think yours is the holocaust.

DORA: Is that how you see it?

VON BRAUN: Well why else are you bothering me with all this. What do you want of me? It was a long time ago. I am involved in space rockets now.

DORA: I am here to interview you. I told you.

VON BRAUN: No no. I think you want my soul.

DORA: Your soul. Have you got one?

VON BRAUN: Come on Miss Maitland you are an intelligent woman. Surely this is not just Jewish revenge? You want to destroy my life, my family everything I have built up here, is that it?

DORA: That moment, when you knew the Russians were coming in from the East and the Americans from the West, you decided to rush to the Yanks and make a deal.

VON BRAUN: What deal?

DORA: No trial. No mention of your past. And in return...?

VON BRAUN: I wanted the moon. Is that so terrible?

MISS AMERICA: Wernher von Braun, take us to the stars!

VON BRAUN: Coming Miss America

DORA: This is what you want?

VON BRAUN: Goodbye Miss Maitland. Or should I say Goodbye Dora Rosenberg. I think you have enough for your newspaper.

DORA: And when I go to print with the truth about Wernher Von Braun?

VON BRAUN: Why can't you all leave me alone? What do you want me to do? Watch all this go up like a Roman candle. Cancel science?

Scene 24

Pleasing God.

Lights fade gradually as we hear a sound mix of St Matthew's Passion, the Internet, 'you've got mail', The Apollo Moon landing in 1969, the countdown, ten, nine, eight, seven, six, five, four, three, two, one. We have lift off!!! which mix with the Mozart. The cast climb as if going into a rocket. There is smoke, giving the double image of people being gassed and people going to the moon.

As lights go to blackout VON BRAUN returns to childhood and plays joyfully with his rocket as DORA looks up as if watching the Apollo go up to the moon.

Blackout.